Befehlspanzer

German command, control and observation armored combat vehicles
in World War Two – Part 1: tanks of German origin

Contents

– Introduction	2
– Command tanks on Pz.Kpfw.I chassis	12
– Command tanks on Pz.Kpfw.II chassis	22
– Command tanks on Pz.Kpfw.III chassis	25
– Command tanks on Pz.Kpfw.IV chassis	51
– Command tanks on Pz.Kpfw.V chassis	60
– Command tanks on Pz.Kpfw.VI chassis	77
– Appendix	88

ISBN : 978-88-95011-08-0

Text: Riccardo Niccoli
Colour profiles: Jean Restayn © 2014

Acknowledgments and photo credits:
Australian War Memorial (AWM), Bundesarchiv Bildarchiv Koblenz (BA), Hilary Louis Doyle, La Libreria Militare Milan, Jean Restayn (JR), Janusz Ledwoch (JL) – Wydawnictwo Militaria (WM), The Tank Museum Bovington (TMB), US National Archives and Records Administration (US NARA).

RN Publishing S.a.s. di R. Niccoli & C.
Via Torelli 31
28100 – Novara – Italy
Tel. & Fax. +39-0321-455108
www.rnpublishing.com

Graphics and layout: Mauro Martinengo - Novara
Printing: Italgrafica - Novara

© Copyright 2014 – RN Publishing S.a.s.
All rights reserved. No part of this publication may be copied, reprinted or reproduced or used in any form or by any means without written permission by the Publisher.

The colour profiles published in this book are not to scale

cover: A *Befehlspanther* from *I/Pz.Rgt.4* taken in Tuscany, in summer 1944. Note the lack of the coaxial machine-gun in the gun mantle, and the star antenna in the background.
(BA – 101I-478-2167-09 – Bayer)

back cover: A *Pz.Bef.Wg. Ausf.H* from *Stab Pz.Rgt.18, 18. Panzer-Division*, modified as *Tauchpanzer* (amphibious tank), taken while fording the river Bug at Patulin. Russia, June 1941.
(AWM 044596)

Introduction

In the 1930s, it was already clear to some of the most competent and visionary officers that the tank (as the tracked armored combat vehicle become known in Great Britain, the country that was the first to develop and use it on the front, in September 1916) was the weapon of choice for future wars. If World War I had been mainly a static conflict of attrition, due to the lack of adequate means of assault and transportation, the wars of the future would have been featured by dynamic, quick and aggressive operations, thanks to the progress made in the fields of ground, air and naval transportation. Military thinkers such as James Fuller and Basil Liddell Hart in Great Britain, Charles De Gaulle in France, Michajl Tuchacevskji in Soviet Union, all had a clear view of these new strategies of war. However, the most famous theorist of this new doctrine was Heinz Guderian, a German Colonel which in the years 1927-1933 developed his idea of *Blitzkrieg*, or "Lightning War", which had to be made possible by the massive and concentrated use of armored formations, supported by an assault aviation, and

▶ *A kl.Pz.Bef.Wg. from an unidentified Panzer-Division taken during the attack to Poland, in September 1939. The 2 m pole antenna is in raised position, while of the right of the superstructure the markings were cancelled by the censor.* (BA – 101I-318-0083-29-Rascheit)

▲ *An armoured column of the 24. Panzer-Division taken while advancing to Stalingrad, in September 1942. In the foreground, the commander of a Pz.Bef. Wg. Ausf.H controls the presence of possible threats.* (BA-101I-218-0510-22-Thiede)

▶ *Tanks from 5. Panzer-Division taken in a Polish town, at the end of operation "Fall Weiss", the invasion of Poland, in October 1939. On the right is a kl.Pz.Bef.Wg., showing as markings only the big white crosses, typical of that campaign.* (US NARA)

▼ *A Pz.Bef.Wg. Ausf.E from Pz.Rgt.1, of 1. Panzer-Division, taken on the road to Besancon, France, in June 1940, during operation "Fall Gelb".* (US NARA)

coordinated by a complex network of radio communications.

The seize of power by Adolf Hitler, in 1933, accelerated all the German plans of rearmament, and two years later, when the *Fueher* banned the Versaille Treaty, the real reconstruction of the German Armed Forces (*Wehrmacht*) started. In 1935, the first organic plans for the build up of the German armored force (*Panzerwaffe*) where set up and introduced. The expansion program for the creation of the *Panzerwaffe* went into effect on 15 October 1935; on that date the cover names for the first three armored divisions (*Panzer-Division*) were dropped. Even if the *Panzerwaffe* was still in an embryonic condition, it was quite clear to the German planners that the *Blitzkrieg* would have been feasible only if it was possible to set up a good coordination between the tank commanders and their units, at all levels. Several reports written at the end of the first exercises which involved the first tanks (*Panzer*), clearly remarked that the commanders had the need to stay close to the spearhead of their units, and that they absolutely needed armored vehicles for command and control duties. Thus, it was of capital importance to design and build not only modern tanks equipped with radio sets (and this was quite a modern feature for the time), but also specific and dedicated versions for command and control. In August 1935, the first secret exercise involving an armored division took place. At that time, the only tank in service was the *Panzerkampfwagen I* (*Pz.Kpfw.I*) a small armored vehicle of only 5.4 tons, with a crew of two, and armed with two 7.92mm machine-guns. This light tank was equipped with a radio set, but only capable to receive, and not to transmit; this vehicle was too small to accommodate the required radio sets. So Daimler-Benz developed various solutions to solve the problem. The very first command tank (*Befehlspanzer*) was the *leichte (Funk) Panzerwagen*, 15 of them having being produced on the basis of the *Pz.Kpfw.I Ausfuehrung A* (model A) chassis. They were fitted with one radio transmitter set, plus one radio receiver, but still had a crew of only two. Later, from the same basis it was developed a better variant, the *kleiner Befehls-Panzerwagen*, which offered more internal room to the crew of three, the possibility to observe the battlefield from inside with hatches closed, and the possibility to defend itself, thanks to the presence of a machine-gun in the frontal armor plate.

In 1935 the *Wehrmacht* established the first three *Panzer-Division*, and in December of the same year, it was already defined that the Headquarters (*Stab*) of each armored battalion (*Panzer-Abteilung*) and each armored regiment (*Panzer-Regiment*) had to be equipped with two *Befehlspanzer*. In January 1936, Gen. Beck proposed that a *Befehlspanzer* had to be assigned also to each company commander. These were just plans for the future, as in that period the German industry was struggling to build up its capability to produce basic armaments in large numbers. But those needs would not be forgotten. In 1936,

◀ Not always the commanders rode in command tanks: Here is Oberstltn. (Lt.Col.) Koppenburg, commander of I/Pz.Rgt.1 taken in his tank, a standard Pz.Kpfw.IV coded "'101". Belfort, June 1940. (US NARA)

▼ A Pz.Bef.Wg. Ausf.E from 7. Panzer-Division taken on the French coast of the Channel, in June 1940. Note the code "B01" (in red outlined white), meaning that probably it was assigned to Nachrichten Abteilung 83. (US NARA)

a new model of command tank was developed: the *grosse Befehls-Panzerkampfwagen*. This was based on the *PzKpfw.III* tank, a bigger and better armored vehicle, more suited to be used as combat command post by the high commands. It was completed in three different radio configurations, and was featured by a fixed turret, and by a frame antenna fitted on the engine deck; the armament, however, was still limited to a single machine-gun. At the end of 1936, a contract was placed for the acquisition of 180 *kl.Bef.Pz.Wg.*, plus 30 *gr.Bef.Pz.Wg*. These were the two command tanks (of German design) with which the *Panzerwaffe* entered the war, on September 1, 1939. It must be recalled that, starting in 1938, the *Wehrmacht* began to operate also tanks of Czechoslovakian origin, the *Pz.Kpfw.35(t)* and *38(t)*, and their command versions, but these are out of the aims of this book, which is dedicated only to the command tanks of German design.

At the start of the Poland campaign (operation *"Fall Blue"*), the *Panzerwaffe* had a total of 215 *Panzer-Befehlswagen* (180 *kleine* and 35 *grosse*), with 177 of them assigned to the combat units. This campaign was relatively easy for the *Wermacht*, and only 13 command tanks were hit during the combats, five of them being completely destroyed. On May 10, 1940, for operation *"Fall Gelb"*, the attack to France, Belgium and the Netherlands, the *Panzer-Befehlswagen* force was formed by 244 vehicles, on a total of more than 3,400 tanks. In this case, the combats were more demanding, as it is clear analyzing the losses: in total, 69 command tanks were lost in less than two months of fighting. The feedbacks of these two first *Blitzkrieg* were already clear. The command tanks proved to be an excellent tool for the *Panzerwaffe*, but they absolutely needed a traversable turret, and they had a really insufficient armament. Even at this point of the war, in some cases personnel of the combat units proposed to field-modify some tanks (*Pz.Kpfw.III*) to operate as command tanks, by simply adding the necessary radio sets, and fitting the extendable antenna mast to the outside of the tank. In order to improve the situation, a new type of command tank was developed, now featured by a 5 cm gun and a traversable turret,

▶ *A kl.Pz.Bef.Wg. from the Trupp of the* Minenraum-Abteilung 1, *taken during operation "Barbarossa", in Russia, July 1941. Note the special frame antenna, fitted to improve the long range communications of the radio set. See profile at page 20.* (BA-101I-265-0007-02-Mossdorf)

▼ *Three Pz.Bef.Wg. Ausf.H from Pz.Rgt.36, of* 14. Panzer-Division, *taken in Ukraine, in August 1941, while the rest of the Regiment passes alongside. The command tanks were always in close contact with the combat units they controlled.* (US NARA)

▼▼ *A Pz.Bef.Wg. Ausf.H, probably from* 21. Panzer-Division, *taken in Libya, in spring 1942. Note the two big stowage boxes fitted to the rear. Room was never enough in the command tanks.* (US NARA)

◀ A number of Pz.Kpfw.II were converted on the field to command duties. This Ausf.C *"104"*, from I/Pz.Rgt.21, of 20-Panzer-Division, *taken in 1942, was probably one of them. Note the presence of an observation periscope near the open turret hatch.* (Schick via JR)

▼ *A Pz.Bef.Wg. Ausf.J code "555" from Stab II/SS-Pz.Rgt. "LSSAH" taken at Kharkov, in March 1943. Note that the photographer avoided to take the rear part of the tank, in order to hide the new star antenna, which identified the command tanks. See profile at page 42.* (BA-101III-Cantzler-067-14)

as the operational tanks. This was the *Pz.Bef.Wg. Ausf.J*, which was ordered as prototype only in 1941, and was assigned to the combat units in 1942. A much improved model was the *Pz.Bef. Wg. Ausf.K*, which adopted a specific new traversable turret armed with the 5 cm KwK.39 (L/60). This *Panzer-Befehlswagen* was produced in late 1942, but only in 50 samples.

In the meantime, on June 22, 1941, Hitler launched his most hazardous and dangerous campaign, operation "Barbarossa", which proved to be the beginning of the end for its *III Reich*, and the worst nightmare for its armed forces, and for the *Panzerwaffe* in the specific. At that time, the *Wehrmacht* could field some 330 *Panzer-Befehlswagen*, largely of Pz.Kpfw.III model, while the command tanks had been retired from the company command level, as the *Panzer* of the Company staff had now both receiving and transmitting radios (Fu 2 and Fu 5 sets). As the *kleiner PanzerBefehlswagen* was gradually replaced by those on the PzKpfw.III chassis, some of them were re-assigned to other units, including Panzer Artillery regiments. In fact, the offensive doctrine of the *Wehrmacht* required that also the artillery fire observation teams had to stay in close contact with the armored spearheads, in order to quickly direct the fire when and where it was required. In early 1943, with the introduction into service of the *Wespe* and *Hummel* self-propelled guns, specifically designed for the *Panzer* units, the *Panzer-Artillerie* would be equipped with dedicated observation tanks (*Beobachtungspanzer*), created from the basis of older models of *Pz.Kpfw. III*, transformed by the industry.

The combats in Russia raised new problems, such as the quality of the transmissions on the long distances in which the units were spread, that created problems in the distribution on time of the orders, and in the coordination of the forces in attack and in defense tactical situations. The level of the threat, especially facing effective enemy tanks, such as the KV-1 and the advanced T-34, was much higher than in the 1940 battles, and it was not uncommon that even the *Befehlspanzer* founded themselves involved in the combats. The need to arm also the command tanks with a gun became paramount, as well as the opportunity to conceal the identity of the *Befehlspanzer*, with the removal of the frame antenna. In this period, as safety measure, some commanders started to prefer to ride in normal combat tanks, leaving the *Befehlspanzer* only to operate as radio relay stations. In some cases, due also to combat losses, some *Pz.Kpfw.III* and *IV* were already modified by the field maintenance units into command tanks, with the installation of radio equipment in standard combat tanks. With the introduction of the *Pz.Bef.Wg. Ausf.J*, the problem posed by the frame antenna was solved: the big and clearly visible frame structure on the engine deck was replaced by a single *Sternantenne* (star antenna), at the rear of the engine deck, which made the command tank identical to the other tanks from distance. Since late 1942-early 1943, the star antenna started to replace the frame antennas in all the command vehicles of the German Army.

The production of the *Panzer-Befehlswagen* was not continuous: it was stopped from March to October 1940, and from February to November 1942. As a result, their number declined; for example, there were only 248 command tanks available in September 1942.

In winter 1942-1943, the *Panzerwaffe* underwent a major reorganization. No more new unit were activated, but it

6 • Befehlspanzer

▶ A Pz.Beob.Wg.III, *probably from SS-Panzer-Division "Das Reich" or "Totenkopf", taken during the battle of Kursk. This was the first combat operation in which the new* Pz.Beob.Wg.III *were used. Note on the rear engine deck the presence of a* Sternantenne D *and of a box, dedicated to stowage special equipmemnt.* (US NARA)

▼ *The* SS-Pz.Rgt."Das Reich" *taken during the battle of Kursk, in July 1943. On the left a column of* Pz.Kpfw.IV Ausf.G *advanced, while on the right side some command tanks were resting, coordinating the attack.* (US NARA)

was decided to strengthen those already in service, or to re-form those decimated or destroyed in the recent battles, and especially in the Stalingrad siege. The *Panzerkampfwagen IV* gradually became the most important and widespread combat tank, but no dedicated *Befehl* version was developed, the *Pz.Bef.Wg.III* of the various models still being the base for the command tanks. The first *Panzer-Befehlswagen IV* did appear in 1941-42, but they were only field modifications created by the units. However, in spring 1943 a new tank appeared in the *Panzerwaffe*, the *Pz.Kpfw.V Panther*. For this vehicle, in the plans destined to become the backbone of the *Panzer-Division*, a *Befehl* version was designed and produced since the beginning. At the same time, since January 1943, a command version was created also for the only heavy tank of the *Wehrmacht*, the *Pz.Kpfw.VI Tiger*. It was clear then, that the *Panzer-Befehlswagen* was not only and no more a special tank to be hidden or preserved, but in the new needs of the war, it

evolved in a tank capable to take part to the combats as the other tanks, with really small differences from the combat versions, in order to ease production standards of the industry, and to allow the field maintenance units to quickly replace the losses with field modifications of standard tanks.

The battle of Kursk, in July 1943, was probably the apex of the *Panzerwaffe* combat capability. Losses in tanks and – above all – in skilled and experienced crews, would not be really replenished in the following years. In October 1943 the number of available *Befehlspanzer* reached its top: 416 vehicles were counted at the combat units. They were formed by versions of all types on the chassis of the *Pz.Kpfw.III*, including field modifications of *Pz.Kpfw.III Ausf.L* and *M*, plus *Pz.Kpfw.IV* modified on the field, *Pz.Kpfw.V*, and *Pz.Kpfw.VI*. However, the losses on the Eastern front, coupled to the impossibility of the German industry to replenish the unit at least on a one-versus-one basis, gradually reduced the strength of the *Panzer* units. At the beginning of 1944, a new organization was defined. The *"Panzerdivision 1944"* included a reduced number of tanks, divided between two battalions, one on *Pz.Kpfw.IV*, and the other on *Panther* tanks. This was only the theory, as on the field the situation was often quite different. The new organization included a total of nine command tanks for the division, divided between three for each *Stab* in the *Regiment* and in the two *Abteilung*. The period June-August 1944 saw the defeat of the *Panzerwaffe* both on the Eastern front, and on the new Normandy front. As a stop-gap measure, the *Wehrmacht* decided (with an arguable decision) to set up new *Panzer-Brigade*, instead of quickly rebuild the battered *Panzer-Division*. These new units, poorly trained and badly balanced, were rapidly dispatched to the front lines, and – as a logical consequence – with the same velocity they were in the most wiped out. In that period a last tank model appeared in the Germany inventory, the *Pz.Kpfw.VI Tiger Ausf.B*, or *Koenigstiger*, the heaviest tank of the war. Also for this model a command version was envisaged since the beginning, but only in few numbers, and the heavy tanks battalions very seldom had the full complement of three *Befehlstiger* in their rows. With the greatly reduced number of *Befehls* and *Beobachtungs Panzer III* available, new versions for these duties were designed from the basis of the *Pz.Kpfw.IV* chassis. They appeared on the front in autumn 1944. In October 1944, the combat units were still fielding a total of 271 command tanks. That was the last time that such a report was completed.

The last re-organization of the *Panzer-Division* appeared in early 1945,

▶ *This* Befehlstiger *from 8./SS-Pz.Rgt."Das Reich", code "S01" was taken during the battle of Kursk. Note the presence of two radio antennas, even if that of the right is not a star antenna. On left of the rear plate is present also the tube containing the additional antenna sections, used for long range communications.* (US NARA)

▲ Befehlspanzer *"I02" from Stab of I/Pz.Rgt.25, 7. Panzer-Division, taken during the battle of Kursk. This was a standard* Pz.Kpfw.III Ausf. L *transformed into command tank on the field. Note the presence of both the MG.34 machine-guns in the hull and in the turret. See profile at page 46.* (BA-101I-022-2922-14-Kipper)

8 • *Befehlspanzer*

▶ *A Pz.Bef.Wg.IV Ausf.G from an unknown Panzer unit, taken on the eastern front in July 1944. The tank was badly hit on the front corner of the turret, and part of the turret Schuerzen was missing, but German personnel was working to recover it. Note the presence of a star antenna on the rear right corner of the hull. (BA-101I-155-2112A-38A-o. Ang.)*

▼ *This Befehlspanzer coded "001" (nicknamed "Brigitte") probably belonged to Pz.Art.Rgt.103 from 4. Panzer-Division, and was taken in September 1944, in Latvia, during operation "Caesar". This was a standard Pz.Kpfw.III Ausf.L field modified to become a command/observation tank. See profile at page 50. (BA-101I-281-1106-04-Petraschk)*

when the number of available tanks was more and more shrinking, and the organization with two tank battalions in a *Panzer-Regiment* was no more feasible. Within this last structure, only four command tanks had to be assigned to each *Regiment*. Even if the command and control duties were no less important in a war that was only reduced to desperate defensive battles, the primary need was then to have combat tanks in the front line, and the *Befehlspanzer* were used in the last months of the war just as they were standard tanks.

Camouflage

Very few words must be spent on the camouflage of the *Befehlspanzer*, as they received the same treatment of all the other tanks of their units. A large number of excellent studies on the German WWII tank camouflage have already been published in the recent years, and we think it's not necessary to spend here too many words on this matter. We simply remember the general official regulations issued during the period 1935-1945.

- Three-tone camouflage: 1935 - 19 July 1937. This scheme (called *Buntfarbenanstrich,* or colorful paint pattern) adopted the RAL colors Nr.17 *Erdgel-matt,* Nr.18 *Braun-matt,* and Nr.28 *Gruen-matt,* taken from the RAL *Farbtoncarte.* They were applied in patches with irregular edges. The patterns had to be different from tank to tank.

- Grey-brown camouflage: 19 July 1937 - 12 June 1940. This scheme adopted the colors Nr.46 *Dunkelgrau* and Nr.45 *Dunkelbrown.* The main color was *Dunkelgrau,* which had to cover 2/3 of the total surfaces.

- Grey camouflage: 12 June 1940 - 18 February 1943. This scheme adopted one single color overall, Nr.46 *Dunkelgrau,* which according to the new RAL numbering system adopted on 10 February 1941, was designated RAL 7021.

- *Afrika* camouflage: 17 March 1941 - 25 March 1942. This scheme adopted *Gelbbraun* RAL 8000 as primary color (on 2/3 of the vehicles), and *Graugruen* RAL 7008 as secondary colour. From 25 March 1942 until the end of the operations in Africa, these two colors were replaced by *Braun* RAL 8020 (2/3 of the vehicles), and *Grau* RAL 7027.

- Sand yellow camouflage: from 18 February 1943 until the end of the war. All the vehicles had to be paint-

ed in *Dunkelgelb nach Muster* (from 3 April 1943 identified as *Dunkelgelb* RAL 7028). Additional colors, to be used by the single units according to the environment conditions, were the *Olivgruen* RAL 6003, and *Schokobraun* RAL 8017. On 19 August 1944 it was ordered that all the combat vehicles had to receive a complete camouflage scheme directly by the factory, and this was different from type to type, and from factory to factory. At the beginning, it was used the *Hinterhalt-Tarnung* (popularly called after the War "ambush camouflage"), soon replaced by other less complicated schemes. In October 1944 and February 1945 other colors appeared: two different tones of the RAL 7028, two different tones of green (*Resendagruen* RAL 6011), and one red-brown (*Rotbraun* RAL 8012).

Of course, a huge number of variations to these orders appeared on the field, especially during wintertime (with improvised whitewash schemes) and in the period of transition from one color scheme to the following. However, simply refer to the various profiles included in this book to have the necessary details.

MARKINGS

A different question concerns the marking in use for the command tanks, as they were conceived just to recognize these precious vehicles within their own unit in combat.

At the beginning, with the *kleiner (Funk) Panzerbefehlswagen*, a complex system made of numbers and symbols was studied; this was applied under an order from *Kommando der Panzertruppen* from 1 June 1937. The markings were usually painted on the driver's front plate, and repeated on a

◀ *A Pz.Bef.Wg.V Panther Ausf.A coded "01" from the* Stab *of Pz.Rgt. "Grossdeutschland", taken in June 1944 on the eastern front. Note the antenna for the Fu 5 radio on the rear of the turret roof. The second from left was* Oberst *Willy Langkeit, Commander of Pz.Rgt. "GD" from March 1943 until October 1944. (BA-101I-712-0498-34-Scheerer)*

▲ *Some kl.Pz.Bef.Wg. served until late in the war. This one, nicknamed "Tiger", belonged to 4. Panzer-Division, and was taken on the eastern front, in summer 1944. On the left there is Pz.Bef.Wg.V Panther "R02", from the* Stab *of SS-Pz.Rgt.5. See profile at page 69. (Muzeum Wojska Ploskiego via WM)*

▶ A Befehlstiger *coded "A", which belonged to* s.H.Pz.Abt.507, *taken probably in summer 1944, on the eastern front. Note the 2 m pole antenna on the turret roof, and the* Sternantenne D *on the right side of the hull.* (copyright reserved, via JR)

▼ *A column of* Panther *tank of an unknown unit taken in Hungary, near the Donau river, in January 1945. In the foreground is a Befehlspanther Ausf.G, featured by a pole antenna on the turret roof, and by a* Sternantenne D *on the rear of the engine deck. On the rear plate, on the left side of the right stowage box, it's possible to see the connections for the installation of the additional antenna sections for the Fu 8 radio set.* (Knirsch via JR)

placard carried on the rear. With the introduction into service of the *kleiner Befehlspanzer*, and with the broke out of the war, at the end of August 1939 another type of codification was introduced. All the tanks in a unit had to be identified by a three-digit system, in which the first digit indicated the Company, the second digit the Platoon in the Company, and the third digit the single tank in the Platoon. This codification was applied painting the numbers on the sides (and often on the back) of the turret, or (in the first months of war) fitting small black metal placards to the sides and back of the hull. At this stage, the command tanks were identified thanks to a variation to the three-digit system, in which in place of the Company number appeared a letter, an "R" for tanks in the Regimental staff, a "B" for tanks in the Brigade staff, and a Roman digit ("I", "II" or "III") in case of tanks in the *Abteilung* staffs. Other codifications included the letter "D" (probably for *Division*), but there were also codes such as "RN" (*Regiment Nachtricht,* or regiment signal) or "IN" (1st battalion *Nachricht*). To explain the reasons of all these variations, it is useful to remember that in a *Panzer-Division* the *Befehlspanzer* were not assigned only to the *Stab* of the *Panzer-Regiment* or of a *Panzer-Abteilung*. A number of command tanks were also assigned to the *Nachrichten-Abteilung*, the divisional radio and communication battalion, one of the most important units of the *Division*, especially in waging offensive operations. In 1940, the *Nachrichten-Abteilung* was formed by two main elements: the *Nachrichten-Kompanie*, and the *Panzer-Funk-Kompanie*, which operated a mix of communications cars and trucks (*Kfz.2, 15, 17, and 77*), radio armored cars (*SdKfz.260, 261* and *263*), and up to seven *Befehlspanzer III*. Usually, the first platoon of the *Panzer-Funk-Kompanie* was attached to the Division Headquarters, the second platoon was attached to the *Schuetzen-Brigade* HQ (together with a radio section from the *Nachrichten-Komp.*), and the third platoon was attached to the *Panzer-Brigade* (or *Panzer-Regiment*) HQ. In 1942-43, the *Nachrichten-Abteilung* saw a reduction in command tanks to only three *Befehlspanzer III*, while there was a remarkable increase in radio and communication armored half-tracks: up to 39 *SdKfz.251* of the /3, /6, and /11 versions. In 1944-45, the number of radio armored vehicles in the *Nachrichten-Abt.* was drastically reduced by the problems of war, and only two *Befehlspanzers* and 16 *SdKfz.251* of various versions were (in theory) assigned.

During the war, in order to try to protect the command and control tanks from enemy fire, other systems were developed, using above all numbers in the "zero" series, such as "0", or "01" or "001", but also letters, such as "K" (for *Kommandeur*, or *Kommandant*), and "AJ" (for *Adjutant*). In other cases, it was decided to use odd numbers, representing tanks not normally present in the unit, such as "901" (in a Regiment with no more than eight Companies), "501" or "555" (in a Battalion with no more than four Companies), or "154" (when a fifth Platoon in the first Company didn't exist). The *Beobachtungspanzer*, on the other hand, were usually marked with the letter "A" (for *Artillerie*), "AR" (for *Artillerie-Regiment*) or "B" (probably for *Beobachtungs*) with or without numbers. In other cases, also other letters were used, such as "C" or "J". It must be recalled that also the reconnaissance Platoons of the Panzer units sometimes made use of letters, usually the "A" before the numbers, meaning *Aufklaerungs*. However, in such cases the tanks were standard combat vehicles, and not *Befehl* or *Beobachtung Panzers*. ❏

Pz.Kpfw.I chassis

The very first "modern" Panzer to be introduced into service by the *Wehrmacht* was the *M.G. Panzerwagen* (designated from 3 April 1936 *Pz.Kpfw.I Ausf.A*), which started to be delivered to the armoured units in 1934. As a logical choice, the first command tank was then built on that chassis. It was just an experimental vehicle, built in only 15 samples. They were called *leichte (Funk) Panzerwagen mit Sonderaufbau* (or light radio tanks with special superstructure). The main external feature of these vehicles was the presence of a fixed superstructure in place of the traversing turret, destined to provide more room for the commander and the driver. The chassis were selected from the 2.Serie/La.S. production lot. The superstructure housed on the right rear corner a 2 meters pole antenna, which could be lowered towards the front of the tank, in a position which was protected by a frame mounted on the right track guard. The superstructure roof was equipped with one commander's hatch, of semicircular shape, hinged on the right side. Three vision ports were also present, to allow a vision of the battlefield on the front, left and rear sides. It is not know the types of radio sets installed in these tanks, but they had, besides the standard receiving sets, 100 and 30 watt transmitters, which the troops recommended to replace with ultra-short-wave sets, with the same range, in order to avoid interferences from the enemy listening units. These 15 test vehicles were used mainly in the first and secret tactical exercise of the first *Panzer-Division*, that was held at the *Truppenuebungsplatz* at Munster, from 18 to 30 August 1935. These first *Befehlspanzers* were assigned to the Battalion and Company commanders of the I. and II. *Abteilung/Kraftfahrlehrkommando Zossen* (cover name for the I. and II. *Kampfwagen-Abteilung* of *Kampfwagen-Regiment 1*), and of the I. *Abteilung/Kraftfahrlehrkommando Ohrdruf* (cover name for the I. *Kampfwagen-Abteilung* of *Kampfawagen Regiment 2*).

On 30-31 October, and 29 November 1935, *Inspektorat 6* (In.6, the *Wehrmacht* inspectorate for motorized and armoured units) held two meetings, with the aim to decide which type of radio sets had to be selected for the *Panzerkampfwagen* and for the *Befehls-Panzerwagen* tanks. The final target as standard command tank was the command version of the *3.7 cm Gesch.Pz.Kpf.Wg.* (which in 1936 will become the *Panzerkampfwagen III*), but since it was too early to make plans for that tank, it was decided to use the *M.G.Pz.Kpf.Wg.* as an interim measure. Then, it was decided to use 72 chassis of the new, lengthened type (later designated *Pz.Kpfw.I Ausf.B*) to

▶ A leichte (Funk) Panzerwagen mit Sonderaufbau, *probably from Kampfwagen Regiment 1, taken in summer 1936. The colour scheme is formed by the three colors (sand, green and brown) introduced in 1935.* (copyright reserved, via JR)

▲ Panzer-Regiment 1 *taken on 29 September 1937, while marching on Charlottenburger Chausse past of the Italian Duce Benito Mussolini, on occasion of his visit to Berlin. The kl.Pz.Bef.Wg. on the left is part of the 2./Serie, with no commander's cupola. Curiously, from this photo the tanks appear to be painted in a single very matt color, but they were in the new grey-brown two colors standard camouflage, introduced in July 1937.* (BA-102-17936-Georg Pahl)

▶ *In 1936-37, Pz.Rgt.1 undertook several tests and trials, in order to increase the range of the command tanks radio sets. Here appear a kl.Pz.Bef.Wg. and a Pz.Kpfw.I Ausf.B modified with large frame antennas, a solution that was not approved for series production. See profile at page 17.* (copyright reserved, via JR)

▼ *A Pz.Kpfw.I Ausf.B (probably from Pz.Rgt.4) with an unusual modification, the integration of a kl.Pz.Bef.Wg. commader's cupola on the standard turret. Possibly a pre-war command tank test.* (Schick via JR)

▼▼ *On the right, a kl.Pz.Bef.Wg., probably from Pz.Rgt.4, taken with a Pz.Kpfw.I Ausf.A during an exercise in Germany, before 1939.* (US NARA)

make available the needed number of command tanks, designated *kleiner Befehls-Panzerwagen*.

On 15 January 1936, a contract was signed for the production of 1,500 M.G. Pz.Kpf.Wg. Of these, 1,175 were Pz.Kpf.Wg.I (MG) with Krupp engine, while 325 had Maybach engine. The 72

command tanks were included in the latter batch of 325. By mid-1936, these tanks received the official designation of *kleiner Panzer-Befehlswagen (Sd. Kfz.265)*. The transformation consisted in the installation of a fixed superstructure, larger than that of the previous model, and now armed with a 7.92mm MG.13 or MG.34 machine-gun. The superstructure housed a crew of three (driver, radio operator, and commander/gunner) plus one radio receiver set, and one 20 watt transmitter set. It was fitted with one two-doors hatch on the roof, plus another two-doors hatch on the left side. The superstructure was made of several high nickel-chromium armor plates welded together. The armour was 13mm thick for the walls, and only 8mm thick for the roof. The lower part of the superstructure had the same vision ports of the *Pz.Kpfw.I Ausf.B*, while the upper part had visors only in the front, right, and rear plates. The machine-gun was fitted to the front right upper corner of the superstructure, in a ball mount. It was aimed thanks to a K.Z.F.1 telescopic sight with 1.8x magnification, and 18 degree field of view. The ammunition reserve was formed by 12 double-drum magazines housing 75 rounds of *SmK* of *SmK L'Spur* type (cased or tracing) each, for a total of 900 rounds.

According to the radio equipment designation system, introduced on 1 October 1937, the radio set consisted of one transmitting/receiving *Funkgeraet 6* (Fu 6, SE20u and Eu) 20 watt ultra short-vawe set, mounted in racks in the left rear of the superstructure, plus one receiving Fu 2 (EU) ultra short-vawe set, mounted in a rack right of the driver. The 2 meters pole antenna associated to the Fu 6 was located on the rear right corner of the superstructure, and when not in use, it could be lowered in a protective sloped rail, fitted to the right mudguard. The Fu 6 had a voice range of 3-6 km.

The *kleiner Panzer-Befehlswagen* were all assembled by Daimler-Benz at the Werk 40 factory, and first deliveries occurred in July-August 1936. By 1 October, 40 tanks resulted delivered to the Panzer units. This model proved to be effective, and already in September 1936 a new contract for 108 additional kl.Pz.Bef.Wg. was issued, all to be delivered by the end of 1937. To this total of 180 tanks, four more were produced when four previous samples were assigned to the Condor Legion in Spain.

According to the *Kriegsstaerkenach-weisungen* (K.St.N., or wartime organization table) 1194, 1168, 1195, 1171 and 1175 of 1 October 1937, the *kl.Pz. Bef.Wg.* were assigned one to each Panzer-Kompanie (Tank Company),

◀ The special modified kl.Pz.Bef.Wg. of the Trupp from Minenraum-Abteilung 1 taken during operation "Barbarossa", in July 1941. See profile at page 20. (US NARA)

▼ The late use of the kl.Pz.Bef.Wg. included even its conversion into an armoured moving shooting platform, on behalf of the Propoganda-Kompanie (PK). *This was one from* 11. Panzer-Division, *in Russia, 1942.* (US NARA)

▼▼ A mechanic at work on a kl.Pz.Bef.Wg. of Pz.Rgt.3 at Bruenn, in March 1939, at the end of the invasion of Czechoslovakia. (US NARA)

two to each *Nachrichten-Zug* (Signal Platoon) of the *Panzer-Abteilung* (Tank Battalion), and one to each *leichter Panzer-Zug* (Light Tank Platoon) of each *Panzer-Regiment-Stab* (Tank Regiment HQ). In addition, each *Nachrichten-Abteilung* (Signal Battalion) of the *Panzer-Division* was to receive two of these tanks. With new *K.St.N.*, in late 1939 the presence of the *kl.Pz. Bef.Wg.* in the *Panzer-Regiment* was greatly reduced.

The first operational use of the *kl.Pz. Bef.Wg.* occurred in October 1936, when one of these tanks was shipped in Spain, together with 32 *Pz.Kpfw.I*. This contingent was handed over to Gen. Franco's Spanish Nationalist forces, with their crews being trained by German personnel under Lt.Col. Ritter von Thoma, commander of the so called *Panzerabteilung 88* "Drohne" of the Condor Legion. A total of four

kl.Pz.Bef.Wg. were delivered to Spain during the war, together with 102 Pz.Kpfw.I, about equally divided between Ausf.A and B. No official records can confirm these numbers, as the tanks were given to the Spanish Nationalist forces as a gift, and not sold. The result of the use of these tanks (almost always manned in combat by Spanish crews) was satisfactory under the mechanical reliability point of view; however, their combat capability, especially against the Russian BT-5 and T-26 tanks, proved to be already outdated.

The first *Kl.Pz.Bef.Wg.* were delivered without armament, as there were delays in the production of the ball mount for the machine gun; the hole in the superstructure front was covered with a dedicated plate, until the ball mount were installed, as retrofit.

Other modifications to the *kl.Pz.*

Bef.Wg. were carried out after the delivery to the operational units, some destined to improve the mechanical components, other to increase the combat capabilities. In 1937, a *Nebelkerzenabwurfvorrichtung* (rack for smoke grenades) with five cartridges was mounted on the rear of the tank. In the same year, starting with the late production of the 3.Serie tanks, two pistol loop-holes were added for close defence, one in the left front plate, the other in the right rear plate. In 1938, the *Kl.Pz.Bef.Wg.* were retrofitted with a commander's cupola, produced in two types. The first type maintained the same roof hatch of the superstructure, and was made of 13 mm armour plates. The second type was featured by a rounded signal port in the hatch lid, bullet-proof 90 mm thick glass vision blocks, wider rain/sun guards, and was made of 14.5 mm nickel-free armour plates. In 1939, a *Nachtmarschgeraet* (night march device) was fitted, composed by a Notek blackout light and by a tail light. In 1940, a new cooling system for the engine was introduced. This was approved for a secret project called "Achse", in order to allow the use of the tanks (including the *Pz.Kfpw.I Ausf.B* version) in hot conditions, with temperatures up to 45° C. The *Tropen* (tropic) modification included the change of the ventilation housing, the installation of a new fan wheel coupled to a new double pulley drive, and the increase of the size of the cooling air ducts. These modifications were introduced in February 1941, first for the tanks of *Pz.Rgt.5* (destined to be shipped to North Africa) and *Pz.Rgt.6*.

On 15 August 1939, before the beginning of the Poland invasion, the 180 *kl.Pz.Bef.Wg.* in service were distributed to the following units: 10 vehicles each to *Pz.Rgt.3, 4, 5, 6, 7, 8, 11, 15, 31, 35, 36*; six vehicles each to *Pz.Abt.(verl)33, Pz.Abt.65, Pz.Abt.(verl)66, Pz.Abt.(verl)67*; five vehicles each to *Pz.Rgt. 1, 2, I./Pz.Rgt.10, I./Pz.Rgt.23, I./Pz.Rgt.25*; three vehicles each to *4.Pz.Brig., Pz.Nachr.Abt.77 and 79*; two vehicles each to *Pz.Lehr-Abt., Pz.Nachr.Abt.37, 38, 39*, one vehicle each to *Stb. Pz.Rgt.25* and *Schiesslehrgang*.

The *kl.Pz.Bef.Wg.* remained in service for many years, and some samples where still in front line service in 1944, with the *4.Panzer-Division*, for example. However, since 1940-41 they were obsolete and outclassed, and were gradually replaced by other types of *Panzerbefehlswagen*. Starting in spring 1940, after that most company commanders had received *Pz.Kpfw.III* tanks, some *Sd.Kfz.265* were assigned to the commands of some Panzer Artillery Regiments, to be used by forward observation officers, in order to provide them a full protected vehicle during combat operations in support of the armored formations. The communication set was not changed, and remained composed by one Fu 6 and one Fu 2 radio sets. They were the first tanks used as *Beobachtungspanzer*, or observation tanks, and their first employment dates back to the campaign in the West, in May-June 1940. It is known that *kl.Pz.Bef.Wg.* where assigned in number of 12 to *Art.Rgt. 103 (4.Pz.Div.)*, six to *Art.Rgt.73 (1.Pz.Div.)* and *Art.Rgt.78 (7.Pz.Div.)*, four to *Art.Rgt.74 (2.Pz.Div.)* and *Art.Rgt.116 (5.Pz.Div.)*. Finally, those which were not destroyed or badly damaged in combat, were retired or diverted to other use. Some were assigned to *Panzer-Jaeger* (tank hunter) and *Panzer-Pionier* (armoured engineers) units, some were converted to be operated as armoured ambulances or ammunition carriers,

Kl.Pz.Bef.Wg. Sd.Kfz.265: PRODUCTION LIST

	FIRM	FGST.NR. SERIE	NUMBER
4.A SERIE/LA.S.FAHRGESTELL for 1.SERIE	GRUSONWERK	9406-9430	25
5.A SERIE/LA.S.FAHRGESTELL for 2.SERIE	DAIMLER-BENZ	10478-10497, 10506-10512, 10514-10518, 10522	30
	HENSCHEL	12521	1
	GRUSONWERK	14507-14510, 14515-14517, 14519-14520, 14522-14528	16
7.A SERIE/LA.S.FAHRGESTELL for 3.SERIE	DAIMLER-BENZ	15001-15044	44
	HENSCHEL	15101-15168	68
TOTAL			**184**

Kl.Pz.Bef.Wg. Sd.Kfz.265: SPECIFICATIONS

LENGTH:	4.42 M
WIDTH:	2.06 M
HEIGHT:	1.99 M
WEIGHT (COMBAT):	5.88 T
ENGINE:	MAYBACH NL38 6 CYL. WATER-COOLED 3.8 LT GASOLINE, DELIVERING 100 HP AT 3,000 RPM
FUEL CAPACITY:	146 LT
TRANSMISSION:	ZF FG31, WITH 1 REVERSE AND 5 FORWARD GEAR
MAX SPEED:	40 KM/H
RANGE (ON ROAD):	170 KM
RANGE (CROSS COUNTRY):	115 KM
GRADE:	30°
TRENCH CROSSING:	1.40 M
STEP:	37 CM
FORDING DEPTH:	60 CM
GROUND CLEARANCE:	29.5 CM
GROUND PRESSURE:	0.52 KG/CM2
POWER RATIO:	17 HP/TON
WEAPONS:	1 x 7.92MM MG.34 MACHINE GUN
AMMUNITION:	900
PROTECTION:	SUPERSTRUCTURE AND HULL: 13 MM
COMMUNICATIONS:	1 x FU 6, 1 x FU 2
CREW:	3

◀ This 3./Serie kl.Pz.Bef.Wg. (Fgst.Nr. 15118), code "I03", was captured to the 21. Panzer-Division by the British 8th Army in North Africa, and moved to the UK for evaluation. Today it is on display at the Royal Tank Museum Bovington. This photo was taken in September 1994. (R. Niccoli)

other were assigned to minor tasks, even to the photo and video operator teams of the *Propaganda Kompanien* (PK), in order to provide a safe platform for shooting during combat operations or in dangerous areas.

The *kl.Pz.Bef.Wg.* were also used as radio control vehicles to guide the B II *Minenraeum-Wagen* (*Sd.Kfz.300*), or mine clearing vehicles. A first *Kompanie* on three *Zug* (Platoon) was created on 1 June 1940. It received one *kl.Pz.Bef.Wg* for the *Kompanie-Trupp*, plus three of these vehicles for each of the three Platoons, destined to control nine *Sd.Kfz.300*. On 1 December 1940 the *Minenraum-Kompanie* was expanded into *Minenraum Abteilung 1*, on two Companies, and this unit saw action during Operation "Barbarossa", from 22 June 1941. However, operations in combat were unsatisfactory due to problems of the B II, and on 8 September 1941 the unit was redesignated *Panzer Abteilung (Funklenk) 300*, and later was re-equipped with *Pz.Kpfw.III (5 cm)* and B IV *Sprengladungstraeger* (*Sd.Kfz.301*).

In order to improve the performances of the radio sets, since 1941 some *kl.Pz.Bef.Wg.* received frame antennas (similar in concept to those fitted on the *gr.Pz.Bef.Wg.*), thanks to field-modification works. This was the case, for example, in the *20. Panzer-Division* and in the *Minenraum Abteilung 1*. ❑

LEICHTE (FUNK) PANZERWAGEN MIT SONDERAUFBAU, **KAMPFWAGEN REGIMENT 1**, MUNSTER, AUGUST 1935.

This was one of the 15 very first *Befehlpanzers*, produced on the *M.G. Panzerwagen* chassis, the tank that from 1936 was designated *Panzerkampfwagen I Ausfurung A*. Its colour scheme was the standard adopted by the German armoured units in the period 1935-1937. This scheme adopted the colours Nr.17 *Erdgel-matt*, Nr.18 *Braun-matt*, and Nr.28 *Gruen-matt*, taken from the *RAL Farbtoncarte*. They were applied in patches with irregular edges. The patterns had to be different from tank to tank.

KLEINER PANZERBEFEHLSWAGEN SDKFZ.265,
1.PANZER-DIVISION, GERMANY, JUNE 1937.

This was the early version of the *kleiner Befehlspanzer*, which didn't have the commander's cupola, but only a rectangular hatch on top of the superstructure. The colour scheme is still the three-tone green-sand-brown, in use until July 1937.

KLEINER PANZERBEFEHLSWAGEN SDKFZ.265, PZ.RGT. 1,
1.PANZER-DIVISION, GERMANY, PROBABLY 1938.

This early model *kl.Pz.Bef.Wg.* was modified with a frame antenna as part of a series of test dedicated to increase the transmission range of the radio set. It spots the standard camouflage scheme for the period, formed by Nr.46 *Dunkelgrau* and Nr.45 *Dunkelbraun* colours. No markings were visible.

Befehlspanzer • 17

KLEINER PANZERBEFEHLSWAGEN SDKFZ.265, CODE "R02", STAB PZRGT.36, **4. PANZER-DIVISION**, POLAND, SEPTEMBER 1939.

This command tank wears the standard colour scheme adopted in late 1937, consisting of Nr.46 *Dunkelgrau* and Nr.45 *Dunkelbraun*. The main colour was *Dunkelgrau*, which had to cover 2/3 of the total surfaces. Note the white *Balkenkreutz* and the early version of the 4.PzDiv. marking (in yellow), both painted on the side access hatches of the superstructure. The tank's code is on a black rhomboid metal plate, on the sides and also on the rear of the tank.

KLEINER PANZERBEFEHLSWAGEN SDKFZ.265, CODE "1", STAB **PANZER-ABTEILUNG ZUM BESONDERER VERVENDUNG 40** (PZABT.ZBV.40), NORWAY, APRIL 1940.

This vehicle is camouflaged in the grey-brown colour scheme adopted in the period 1937-1940. Its markings consisted of white outlined *Balkenkreuz* on the sides and on the rear, the unit badge, in yellow, on the side hatches, and a number "1", in white, painted only on the right front side of the superstructure.

KLEINER PANZERBEFEHLSWAGEN SdKFZ.265, CODE "I04", STAB I ABTEILUNG/PZ.RGT.5, **5. LEICHTE-DIVISION**, LIBYA, FEBRUARY 1941.

Even if assigned to the North African theatre, all the vehicles of the *5. Leichte Division* were shipped in the standard *Dunkelgrau* colour. The markings were limited to the only "I04" code, in white outline, on the sides of the superstructure; below the code, there still was, in yellow, the 3. Panzer-Division insignia, to which Pz.Rgt.5 belonged until 15 February 1941.

KLEINER PANZERBEFEHLSWAGEN SdKFZ.265, CODE "04", STAB PZ.RGT. 15, **11. PANZER-DIVISION**, RUSSIA, SUMMER 1941.

The colour scheme is *Dunkelgrau* overall, as generally adopted since June 1940. The markings are formed by the German national cross, the *Balkenkreuz*, in white outline only, on the sides and on the rear; the 11. PzDiv. official insigna of that period, a yellow circle, on the left and right front sides of the superstructure; the unofficial badge, the ghost (in white), on the rear sides of the superstructure; and the code "04" in yellow, on the upper left corner of the front plate of the superstructure, and repeated on the right side of the rear plate of the superstructure.

KLEINER PANZERBEFEHLSWAGEN SDKFZ.265, CODE "R02", STAB PZ.RGT.21, **20. PANZER-DIVISION**, RUSSIA, SUMMER 1941.

Colour scheme in *Dunkelgrau* overall. The markings consist of *Balkenkreuz* in black outlined white of the sides of the superstructure and on the left rear plate of the hull; division insigna in yellow on the lower part of the front sides of the superstructure; "R02" code outlined white on the sides and on the rear of the superstructure; black rhomboids with the "R02" code in white, on the sides of the superstructure and over the rear plate of the hull. This tank was modified on the field with the addition of a frame antenna on the engine deck, in order to increase the range of its radio set.

KLEINER PANZERBEFEHLSWAGEN SDKFZ.265, KOMPANIE-TRUPP OF **MINENRAUM-ABTEILUNG 1**, RUSSIA, SUMMER 1941.

Colour scheme *Dunkelgrau* overall. The markings consisted of a single *Balkenkreuz* outlined white on the box fitted to the rear of the superstructure; tactical markings for this unit were painted in white on the left side of the rear hull plate, and on the left front fender. Also this tank was modified on the field with the addition of a large frame antenna, extended over the superstructure and the engine deck, in order to increase the range of its radio set.

KLEINER PANZERBEFEHLSWAGEN SDKFZ.265, PROBABLY STAB PANZER-ARTILLERIE REGIMENT 103, **4. PANZER-DIVISION**, RUSSIA, 1941.

Colour scheme in *Dunkelgrau* overall. The only visible marking was the tactical sign for an artillery unit, painted in white on the left front side of the superstructure, and probably on the rear plate of the hull.

KLEINER PANZERBEFEHLSWAGEN SDKFZ.265, CODE "R", STAB PZ.RGT.8, **15. PANZER-DIVISION**, LIBYA, 1942.

This tank was originally painted in *Dunkelgrau*, and then re-painted in *Gelbbraun* (RAL 8000) overall. The markings include a large "R" code in red on the sides and on the front plate of the superstructure; it was probably repeated on the rear plate. On the front plate there were also the white palm, insignia of the *Afrika Korps*, and the marking of the *15. Panzer-Division*, in red; this was probably repeated on the rear plate of the hull. This tank also had a "loophole" pistol port on the left front side of the superstructure.

Befehlspanzer • 21

Pz.Kpfw.II chassis

Officially, no *Panzer-Befehlswagen* or *Panzer-Beobachtungswagen* were ever designed and produced by the German industry on the *Pz.Kpfw.II* chassis. However, a small number of tanks of the *Ausf.B* and *C* versions were modified in the turret, with the addition of a superstructure that was probably fitted to better accommodate the commanding officer, in its command and control duty. These tanks appear only in a few and rare photos of the period 1938-1940, while operating with other tanks, but showing no additional frame or pole antennas. It is commonly believed they were used as *Befehlspanzer*. Unfortunately, no primary sources or documents exist about this model, sometimes unofficially called "*Mit Umbau*" or "*Mit Aufbau*", and it is not known their exact purpose, which unit operated them, and how many were produced.

A couple of years later, under the needs of a total war, some other modifications were introduced in the *Pz-Kpfw.II* family. Starting in 1942-43, the remaining *Pz.Kpfw.II* tanks still in service, by now completely outdated and outclassed for combat operations, were gradually assigned to secondary roles, such as reconnaissance, training, and conversion to other tasks. Personnel in the German maintenance units was ingenious, resourceful and skilled enough to carry out transformation on the field, in order to fully exploit all the means at disposal of the *Panzer* units. Thanks to the field installation of appropriate radio sets, Fu 4, Fu 5 and Fu 8 in the main, some *Pz.Kpfw.II* were modified for use as command tanks and observation tanks. Photo evidences are known of *Pz.Kpfw.II* from *Afrika Korps* modified

▲ *This photo taken during the battle of Kursk, in July 1943, shows a Pz.Kpfw. II Ausf.F code "914", probably from 12. Panzer-Division (together with a Pz.Bef. Wg.III Ausf.J code "943"). The Pz.II is equipped with a kind of star antenna, indicating that it was field modified to operate with a Fu 8 radio set. See profile at page 24. (BA-101I-022-2924-07-Kipper)*

with three pole antennas. Other were fitted with frame antennas on the engine deck, and used in 1943-44 as *Panzer-Beobachtungswagen* and *Panzer-Befehlswagen* by *Panzer-Artillerie*, *Sturm-Panzer* and *Panzer-Jaeger* units on the Russian and Italian fronts. Other *Pz.Kpfw.II* have been seen modified with *Sternantenne D* (star antenna) for Fu 8 or Fu 4 radio sets in Russia, in July 1943, and even in Normandy, in August 1944. ❑

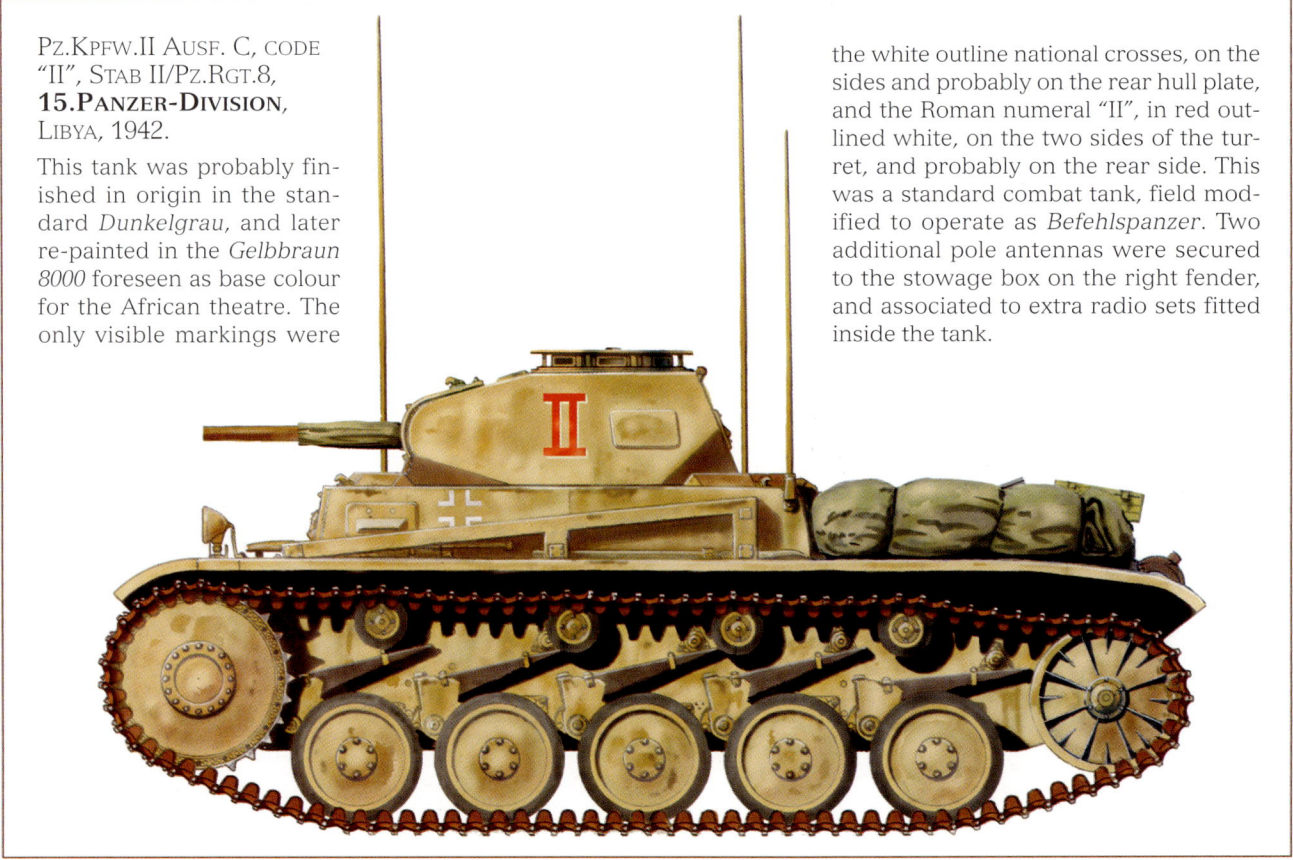

Pz.Kpfw.II Ausf. C, code "II", Stab II/Pz.Rgt.8, **15.Panzer-Division**, Libya, 1942.

This tank was probably finished in origin in the standard *Dunkelgrau*, and later re-painted in the *Gelbbraun 8000* foreseen as base colour for the African theatre. The only visible markings were the white outline national crosses, on the sides and probably on the rear hull plate, and the Roman numeral "II", in red outlined white, on the two sides of the turret, and probably on the rear side. This was a standard combat tank, field modified to operate as *Befehlspanzer*. Two additional pole antennas were secured to the stowage box on the right fender, and associated to extra radio sets fitted inside the tank.

22 • Befehlspanzer

PzKpfw.II Ausf. F, code "AR05", Panzer-Beobachtungs-Batterie 102, Panzer-Artillerie Regiment 102, **9. Panzer-Division**, Russia, summer 1942.

The tank was camouflaged in the standard *Dunkelgrau* overall finish of the period. Its markings include the German national cross, outlined white, on the sides and on the rear hull plate, plus the code "AR05" (probably meaning "*Artillerie Regiment*") in yellow, on the turret sides and rear. This vehicle seems to have no additional radio sets, and thus was used just to provide an armoured mount to the observation officers destined to direct the batteries fire.

PzKpfw.II Ausf. F, code "B01", I/SS-Artillerie-Regiment 3, **SS.Panzer-Grenadier-Division "Totenkopf"**, Ukraine, July 1943.

This vehicle was finished in *Dunkelgelb 7028*, with no additional camouflage colours. Markings were formed by *Balkenkreuz*, black outlined white, on the sides and on the rear hull plate, plus the code "B01" in black, on the turret sides and rear. On the front and probably rear hull plates there were also the temporary divisional markings of the "Totenkopf" for operation "*Zitadelle*", three vertical bars in black. Also this PzKpfw.II seemed to have no additional radio sets, and was used as *Beobachtungspanzer* just as it provided an armoured tracked vehicle to the artillery observation officers who had to follow the armoured formations.

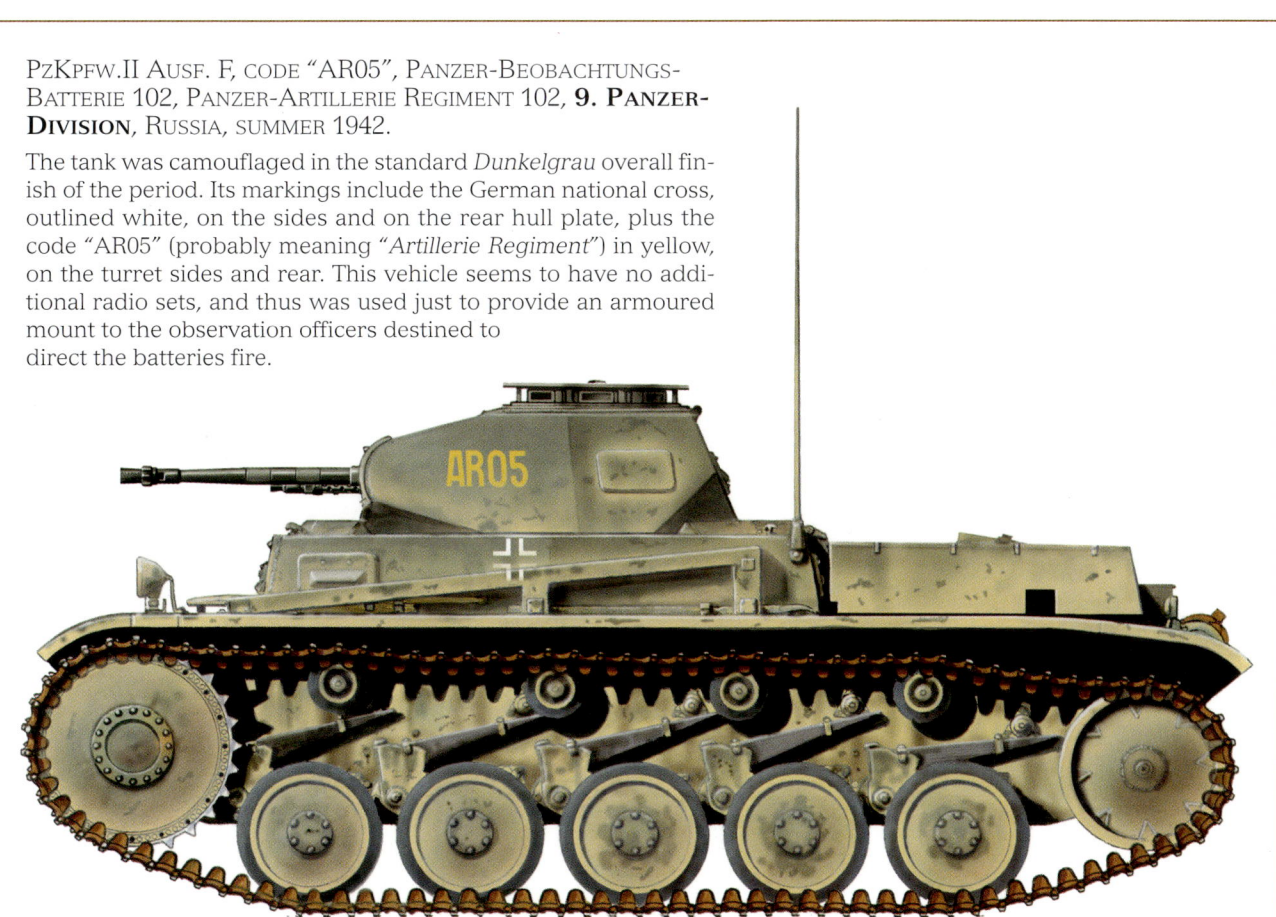

Befehlspanzer • 23

PzKpfw.II Ausf. F, code "914", probably Stab Panzer-Regiment 29, **12. Panzer-Division**, Ukraine, July 1943.

This tank had the standard colour scheme for the period, with *Dunkelgelb 7028* overall, oversprayed with waves and patches of *Olivgruen 6003* and *Schokobraun 8017*. The markings were formed by the German national cross, white outlined, on the sides and on the rear hull plate, plus the code "914", white outlined, on the turret sides and rear. The standard 2 metres pole antenna of this vehicle probably was field modified by adding a kind of *Sternantenne*, indicating that this tank had probably received a Fu 8 radio set.

PzKpfw.II Ausf. C, I/Panzer-Artillerie-Regiment 116, **5.Panzer-Division**, Russia, autumn 1943.

In origin, this tank was delivered in *Dunkelgrau*, but in 1943 it was probably re-painted with a colour scheme formed by a basis of *Dunkelgelb* oversprayed with *Olivgruen*. The markings include the German national cross, in white outline, on the turret sides and rear, plus the division badge, a yellow cross on a black or dark grey square, on the sides. This vehicle was field modified to be operated as *Beobachtungspanzer*, thanks to the introduction of a frame antenna on the engine deck, and the associated Fu 4 radio set. It was also equipped with a large stowage box on the engine deck.

Pz.Kpfw.III chassis

In a meeting held on 30-31 October 1935, the *Wehrmacht Inspektorat 6* decided about the radio communication sets that had to be integrated in the future combat and command tanks. We have already seen that the *kl.Pz.Bef.Wg.* was considered an interim measure, as the command tank which by now fulfilled the needs was that based on the chassis of the Pz.Kpfw.III (at that time still designated *3.7 cm Gesch.Pz.Kpf.Wg.*), and was known as *Fuehrerkampfwagen*.

At the beginning, the plan foresaw to assign two of these vehicles to the *Nachrichten-Zug* (signal platoon) of each *Panzer-Abteilung*, two to the *Nachrichten-Zug* of each *Panzer-Regiment*,

▶ A Pz.Bef.Wg. Ausf.E *from Stab of II/Pz.Rgt.2 of* 1. Panzer-Division, *taken at Bertrix, Belgium, on 12 May 1940, after having skidded into a crater. Note the frame antenna on the engine deck, and the air identification markings: a white cross on the turret roof, and a white band on the engine deck. See profile at page 35.* (US NARA)

▲ A Pz.Bef.Wg. Ausf.D1, *probably from* 5. Panzer-Division, *taken in France, June 1940. Note that the 9 meters Kurbelmast B antenna is extended throught its turret hatch.* (Obzwar-CC-BY-SA-3.0-DE via Wikipedia)

and three to the *Nachrichten-Zug* of each *Panzer-Brigade*. The tank had to be fitted with one (or two in the first case) 20 W ultra short wave transmitters, and two receiving sets. For the *Panzer-Regiment*, one tank had to receive a 30 W transmitter and receiver, while for the *Panzer-Brigade* the tanks with 30 W sets had to be two.

One month later, after another meeting, In 6 decided to correct the specifications. The tank was now designated as *grosser Befehls-Panzerkampfwagen*:

two of them had to be assigned at the *Nachrichten-Zug* of each *Panzer-Abteilung* (equipped with only one 20 W radio set), while seven had to be assigned to the *Nachrichten-Abteilung* of each *Panzer-Division*. The latter had to be divided into five tanks with one 20 W set and one 30 W set, while two were to be fitted with radio set for communication with aircraft and *Luftwaffe* units (*Flieger-Ultrakurzwelle-Sender-Geraet, Flieger-Ultrakurzwelle-Empfaenger, 30 W Sender-Geraet, 30 W Empfanger*).

◀ *A Pz.Bef.Wg. Ausf.E from 4. Panzer-Division, coded "RN1" (in yellow), taken in France, south of Gembloux, in May 1940. In the turret is Oberst (Colonel) Jesse, Commander of Pz.Rgt.36. (US NARA)*

By 3 October 1936, with the introduction of the new designations, the command tank on Pz.Kpfw.III chassis became known as *Panzer-Befehlswagen (Pz.Bef.Wg.)*. In the first years, it was usually called *gr.Pz.Bef.Wg.* to recognize it from the *kl.Pz.Bef.Wg.* The three versions were designated respectively *Sd.Kfz.266, 267* and *268*, according to the type of radio sets installed.

Design and final assembly of the *Pz.Bef.Wg* was assigned to Daimler-Benz, which produced the hull (*Fahrgestell*), and the superstructure (*Panzerkastenoberteil*), while the turret design and production was assigned to Krupp. At the beginning, the new command tank was based on the design of the *Pz.Kpfw.III Ausf.D*.

Panzer-Befehlswagen Ausf.D1

In 1936, *In 6* authorized the production of a first series of 30 *Pz.Bef.Wg.*, which at that time were designated *Pz.Bef.Wg Ausf.A*. They were built between June 1938 and March 1939 at the Daimler-Benz Berlin Merienfelde plant. Only on 7 May 1941 *In 6* decided to rename the designation of the *Pz.Bef.Wg.*, to line them up with the correspondent combat tank version, and in this way avoid confusion. On that date, the *Pz.Bef.Wg. Ausf. A* became *Ausf.D1*, the *Ausf.B* became *Ausf.E*, while the *Ausf.C* was turned into *Ausf.H*. From now onwards, in order to avoid mix up, we will use the late designations of these tanks.

The *Pz.Bef.Wg. Ausf.D1* was significantly different from the *Pz.Kpfw. III Ausf.D*, and it received a dedicated series number, the 3c./ZW. Even if externally similar, the *Ausf.D1* was more than two tons heavier than the combat version (18.2 against 16 tons), thanks mainly to its 30 mm armour plates on all sides of the turret, and on other surfaces. The main feature of this version was the turret, which was bolted to the superstructure, and armed just with a single machine-gun. The front part of the turret had a 30mm curved plate covered by a light metal mantle, featured by a fake 3.7 cm gun and 7.92 machine-gun barrels, while in the right end it housed a ball mount (*MG Kugelblende 30*) for a real 7.92 MG.34 machine-gun, and in the left end a vision port. The MG.34 was aimed thanks to a KZF.2 gunsight with 1.8x magnification with 18° field of view. Ammunition for the MG.34 consisted of 32 drums each containing 75 rounds, for a total of 2,400 7.92mm cartridges. Starting in 1940, the ammunitions were used in belts of 150 rounds, stowed in 16 sacks. Inside the turret, the lack of the gun gave room to the radio sets, and to the crew of five, composed by a *Kommandant* (commander), an *Adjutant* (vice-commander and machine-gunner), a *Panzer-Fahrer* (driver), and two *Panzer-Funker* (radio operators).

The radio equipment of the *Pz.Bef. Wg.* was fitted into dedicated racks, and declined into three versions. In the *Sd.Kfz.266* model it consisted of one Fu 6 (SE20u) with 20 W Sender, and one Fu 2 (Eu). In the *Sd.Kfz.267*, it was formed by one Fu 6 (SE20u) and one Fu 8 (SE30) with 30 W Sender. Finally, the *Sd.Kfz.268* included one Fu 6 (SE20u)

Pz.Bef.Wg. (Sd.Kfz.267 and 268) Ausf.D1 : specifications	
Length:	5.98 m
Width:	2.87 m
Height:	2.41 m
Weight (combat):	18? t
Engine:	Maybach HL108TR V12 Water-cooled 10.8 lt gasoline, delivering 250 HP at 2,800 rpm
Fuel capacity:	300 lt
Transmission:	SSG 76, with 1 reverse and 6 forward gear
Max speed:	39 km/h
Range (on road):	? km
Range (cross country):	? km
Grade:	30°
Trench crossing:	2.60 m
Step:	57.5 cm
Fording Depth:	80 cm
Ground clearance:	37.5 cm
Ground pressure:	0.74 kg/cm2
Power ratio:	13.7 HP/ton
Weapons:	1 x 7.92mm MG.34 machine gun
Ammunition:	2,400
Protection:	Hull (front, sides and rear): 30 mm
	Turret: 30 mm
Communications:	1 x Fu 6, 1 x Fu 8 (SdKfz.267), 1 x Fu 6, 1 x Fu 7 (SdKfz.267)
Crew:	5

▶ *A Pz.Bef.Wg. Ausf.H from Pz.Rgt.36, of 14. Panzer-Division, taken in Ukraina, in August 1941. Note the track section, fitted in front of the turret, as this was fixed.* (US NARA)

▶▼ *A Pz.Bef.Wg. Ausf. E from I/Pz.Rgt.11, 6. Panzer-Division taken in May 1940 near Rotterdam. It had the two pole antennas raised, and the Division markings (two yellow crosses) on the front plate, and on the turret side. The code on the turret was "I03", in white. See profile at page 36.* (US NARA)

▶▼▼ *This Pz.Bef.Wg. Ausf.E (coded "IN3") was operated by Pz.Rgt.31, of 5. Panzer-Division. The photo was taken in Ukraina, in September 1941, after the collapse of a wooden bridge. The tank was equipped with a strange stowage box attached to the turret rear.* (US NARA)

and one Fu 7 (SE20u) *Fliegerboden* Fu, for communications with the aircraft units. The *Ausf.D1* were produced only in the *Sd.Kfz.267* (24 vehicles), and *Sd.Kfz.268* (6 vehicles) configurations. The radio sets were associated to four different antennas, according to their use. At the sides of the superstructure there were two *Stabbantennen* (pole antennas), one 1.4 m long, on the right side, and the other 2.0 m long, on the left side. When not in use, they could be lowered down in protective rails, fitted to the mudguards. On the engine deck it was fitted a removable *Rahmenantenne* (frame antennae), while inside the left side of the turret there was a retractable *Kurbelmast B* (pole antenna), associated on the top to a *Schirmantenne* (star antenna) which could be raised through a circular hatch on the roof of the turret up to a height of 9.0 m.

For observation and surveillance of the battlefield, the *Pz.Bef.Wg. Ausf.D1* was equipped with a twin periscopic *Fahreroptic KFF.1* produced by Ascania, which offered a 1x magnification and 65° field of view. In addition, the commander could use a *Turmspaehfernrohr* (TSF.1), a periscopic traversable binocular which could be raised through the turret roof thanks to a dedicated lid; it had a 3x magnification and 20° field of view. The same opening could also be used to fire signal flares, or use signal flags. In the superstructure there were three vision ports, one to the left of the driver, the other two on the right side, near the radio operator position. The turret had one vision port in the front, and two on the front sides. Finally, the commander's cupola housed five vision slits, which could be opened or closed independently, and were protected by a 90mm thick safety glass.

Befehlspanzer

Pz.Bef.Wg. Sd.Kfz.266, 267, 268 production list					
Series	Ausf.	Sd.Kfz.	Firm	Fgst.Nr. Serie	Number
3c./ZW	D1	267-268	Daimler-Benz	60341-60370	30
4./ZW	E	266-268	Daimler-Benz	60501-60545	45
7./ZW	H	266-268	Daimler-Benz	70001-70175	175
8./ZW	J	266-268	Henschel, Daimler-Benz	73631-73763	81
8./ZW	K	266-268	Daimler-Benz	70201-70250	50
Total					381

Pz.Bef.Wg. Ausf.E

The D1 model was soon followed by an improved version, based on the chassis of the *Pz.Kpfw.III Ausf.E*, which took advantage of the many experiences gathered with the previous model. This was produced by Daimler-Benz between July 1939 and February 1940, in 45 samples, all included in the 4./ZW production series, authorized by *In 6* in July 1938. This batch included all the three versions: *Sd.Kfz.266, 267* and *268*. Externally, the *Pz.Bef.Wg. Ausf.E* was immediately recognizable by the use of a shortened hull, and by the presence of the new and more robust train, formed by six larger wheels on each side, instead of the previous eight. It was featured also by different sprocket wheels (with 20 teeth in place of 21) and idler wheels (reinforced with the addition of eight spokes). Of course many other big and small differences where present, the same as between the *Pz.Kpfw.III Ausf.D* and *E*. The mission equipment, however, were not much different, with the exception of the KFF.1 periscopic sight, which was replaced by a KFF.2 *Fahreroptik*, with a magnification of 1.5x and 50° field of view.

Pz.Bef.Wg. Ausf.H

The final version of the *Pz.Bef.Wg.* family with fixed turret and frame antenna was the *Ausf.H*, ordered (as the *Ausf.E*) in July 1938 in 145 samples, and produced by Daimler-Benz between November 1940 and December 1941. A second contract for further 30 tanks was produced in January 1942. Differences between the *Ausf.E* and the *Ausf.H* were those of the respective standard combat models, and in addition, in the second batch of 30 vehicles, the 3.7 cm fake gun was replaced by a 5 cm dummy gun tube, to make the tank looking like the most recent combat version. During the production run, new cast drive and idler wheels were introduced, as well as an armour protection to the NKAV (smoke grenade launcher) at the rear. On the contrary, since the beginning, this model was equipped with the wider Kgs 61/400/120 tracks, 40 cm wide. Also the commander's cupola was slightly different, with the slides of the vision slits being narrower and much thicker.

Pz.Bef.Wg. Ausf.J

As already mentioned, the feedbacks from the first *Pz.Bef.Wg.* combat experiences resulted above all in the request by the *Panzer* units to produce new vehicles featured by a real anti-tank gun mounted in a traversable turret, and by increased armour protection. These needs were satisfied with the order of a new version of the *Pz.Bef.Wg.*, designed on the chassis of the *Pz.Kpfw.III Ausf.J* (8./ZW series). Again, Daimler-Benz was selected to design the hull and superstructure, while Krupp was charged to develop the turret. The armament to be fitted was the 5 cm KwK.38 (L/42), the same gun which had been installed in the

▲ *This* Pz.Bef.Wg. Ausf.H *coded "I00" belonged to the* Stab *of* SS-Pz.Abt. "Wiking", *from* SS-Division (mot.) "Wiking". *The photo was taken just after the arrival of the unit in Russia, in early May 1942. See profile at page 39.* (US NARA)

◄ *A* Pz.Bef.Wg. Ausf.J *from* SS-Pz. Rgt."Totenkopf" *of* SS-Panzer-Grenadier-Division "Totenkopf", *during the battle for Kharkov, in February 1943. The code on the turret "II01" was white outlined black, while the Division marking, the "Death's Head", was painted in white near the driver's visor.* (Strategia KM via WM)

◀ Nice photo of a Pz.Bef.Wg. Ausf.K (code "RN1") from 4. Panzer-Division, taken in Russia, probably in spring 1943. Note the unusual star antenna, positioned on a very long rod, and fitted to the right hull side, and not on the standard position, on the engine deck. (Schick via JR)

Pz.Kpfw.III since the Ausf.E version. One test vehicle was made ready by August 1941, with mass production scheduled to begin in July-August 1942. For the series production were used 81 standard hulls of Pz.Kpfw. III Ausf.J, produced by Henschel, which were then converted by Daimler-Benz. The conversion included the internal installation of the radio racks destined to house the different sets for the Sd.Kfz.266, 267 or 268 versions, and the installation of a second pole antennae (1.4 m long) on the left side of the superstructure, while the Ausf.J 2.0 m pole antenna on the right side was maintained. The main innovation of this version was the adoption of a new type of antenna, the *Sternantenne D* (star antenna) in place of the previous frame antenna, thanks to the welding of an armoured pot in the middle of the rear part of the engine deck, which protected the insulator upon which the antennae was mounted. The main advantage of the new antennae was that from distance it was barely visible, and the Pz.Bef.Wg. appeared to the enemy's eyes as a standard combat tank. To gain room for the radio sets inside the combat compartment, the *Kugelblende 50* with its MG.34 machine-gun, fitted to the right side of the front hull, was replaced by a *MP-Klappe*, a simple port for the use of pistol or *Maschinepistole* weapons. For the same reason, also the MG.34 mount inside the turret was removed. Other main external features of the Ausf.J compared to the previous models were the presence of 20 mm thick *Vorpanzer*, additional spaced armour on the gun mantel and on the front hull, and new ventilation hoods on the engine hatch lids. The production of the Pz.Bef.Wg. Ausf.J was completed in November 1942. Since September 1942 two *Nebelkerzen-Wurfgeraeten* (smoke grenade dischargers) each made of three tubes loaded with *Schnell-Nebelkerzer 39* cartridges, were retrofitted, to be mounted on the front sides of the turret, using the bolts for the lifting hooks. Finally, since May 1943 these tanks were retrofitted also with the *Schuerzen* (skirts), spaced armour mounted around the turret, and on the hull sides, four plates on each side.

Pz.Bef.Wg. Ausf.K

The final development of the Pz.Bef. Wg. on Pz.Kpfw.III chassis was the Ausf.K, which was designed at the beginning of 1942. This version was conceived to solve all the problems assessed in the previous versions, and provided more protection, better armament and increased internal room than the previous models. The Ausf.K was produced on the basis of the Pz.Kpfw.III Ausf. M chassis, coupled to a turret of new design, which was approved on 15 April 1942. The turret was developed from the *BW.40 Turm*, designed for the Pz.Kpfw.IV, and was mounted on the same *Turmkugellager* (turret ball race) of the Pz.Kpfw. IV Ausf.E. The turret was completely traversable, and was equipped with a 5 cm KwK.39 (L/60) gun, protected by a small *Walzenblende* (gun mantlet), slightly moved to the left. On the right front panel of the turret there was room for one *Beobachtungs-Sehklappe* (observation vision port). The commander's cupola was of new design, and was featured by a single

Pz.Bef.Wg. (5 cm, Sd.Kfz.266-268) Ausf.K : specifications	
Length:	6.16 m
Width:	2.95 m (3.41 with Schurzen)
Height:	2.50 m
Weight (combat):	22? t
Engine:	Maybach HL120TRM V-12 Water-cooled 11.9 lt gasoline, delivering 285 HP at 2,800 rpm
Fuel capacity:	320 lt
Transmission:	SSG 77, with 1 reverse and 6 forward gear
Max speed:	40 km/h
Range (on road):	155 km
Range (cross country):	95 km
Grade:	30°
Trench crossing:	2.30 m
Step:	60 cm
Fording depth:	160 cm
Ground clearance:	38.5 cm
Ground pressure:	0.94 kg/cm2
Power ratio:	13.2 HP/ton
Weapons:	1 x 5 cm Kw.K. (L/60)
Ammunition:	84
Protection:	front: 50+20 mm
Communications:	1 x Fu 8, 1 x Fu 5
Crew:	5

Befehlspanzer • 29

hatch lid, by five vision slits, protected by 90 mm thick glass block, and by the presence of a small metal basket, destined to hold ignited signal flares. At the front of the turret sides, two smoke grenade discharges were fitted. The radio equipment was the same used also on the Ausf.J model, for the Sd.Kfz.266, 267 and 268 types. The antennae set included one star antenna on the engine deck, one 1.4 m pole antenna on the right side of the superstructure (but fitted to the forward part, and folding backwards), and one 2.0 m pole antennae on the left side. To provide room inside the combat compartment, the MG in the hull was removed, and replaced by a pistol port (MP Klappe) as in the Ausf.J. The Ausf.K was produced by Daimler-Benz in only 50 samples, from December 1942 to February 1943. Since May 1943, also this model was retrofitted with Schuerzen around the turret and on the sides of the hull.

At the eve of the war, on 15 August 1939, the 30 gr.Pz.Bef.Wg Ausf. D1 were assigned as follows: two Sd.Kfz.267 each to Pz.Nachr.Abt. 37, 38, and 39; one Sd.kfz.267 each to Pz.Rgt.1, 2, 3, 4, 5, 6, 7, 8, 11, 15, 25, 31, 36, 36, Pz.Nachr.Abt.77, 79, 4. and 6. Pz.Brig.; one Sd.Kfz.268 each to Pz.Nachr.Abt. 37, 38, 39, 77, 79, and 4. Pz.Brig. Unfortunately, following records about the exact assignment of the single command tanks during the war were lost or destroyed. However, Befehlspanzers were assigned to all the panzer units, including the armoured signal platoons and commands of Panzer-Abetilung, Panzer-Regiment, Panzer-Brigade, Pz.Div. Nachrichten-Abteilung, Panzer-Funk companies, Sturmegeschuetz-Abteilungs, Sturmgeschuetz-Brigades, Sturmpanzer-Abteilung, Panzer-Jaeger-Abteilung. According to K.St.N 1194 (Sd.), and 1150 (Sd.), of 1 September 1939, there were two Pz.Bef.Wg.III in the Nachrichten-Zug of each Panzer-Regiment Headquarters, and two in the Nachrichten-Zug of each

▲ A Pz.Beob.Wg.III of an SS-Division taken in July 1943, during the battle of Kursk. Note the horizontal stowage box on the rear engine deck, typical of this model, and the Sternantenne D just in front of it. (US NARA)

▲◄ This Pz.Bef.Wg. Ausf.J coded "555" belonged to the Stab of I/SS-Pz.Rgt. "LSSAH", and it was taken during the battle of Kursk, in July 1943. Note that the antenna on the engine deck is missing the upper "star" section. (US NARA)

▼ A brand new Pz.Beob.Wg.III Ausf.F assigned to II/Pz.Art.Rgt.16 of 16. Panzer-Division, in Italy, summer 1943. (HPTM-Deisenberg Coll. Schick via JR)

◀ *A Pz.Beob.Wg.III from SS-Pz.Gren. Div. "Totenkopf" taken in summer 1943. Note the camouflage of* Olivegruen *stripes on the* Dunkelgelb *basic color, but above all the unusual "J" code on the turret* Schuerzen. *(Fey via JR)*

◀▼ *Two Pz.Beob.Wg.III from 16. Panzer-Division knocked out by the US forces in Italy, in the Salerno area, in September 1943. The tank on the right shows a code "51" on the turret* Schuerzen, *but the left side is missing. See profile at page 48. (US NARA)*

◀▼▼ *A Pz.Bef.Wg.III Ausf.J belonging to the SS-Pz.Art.Rgt.5 of 5. SS-Pz.Div. "Wiking" taken in spring 1944, when the II Abt. was reorganised with self propelled guns. The tank, which – with the exception of the* Balkenkreuz – *showed no markings, was probably used as a Pz.Beob.Wg. (US NARA)*

Panzer-Abteilung HQ. The *Nachrichten-Abteilung* of a *Panzer-Division* was assigned seven *Pz.Bef.Wg.*, to be distributed between the units in need, including the Headquarters of the *Panzer-Division*, of the *Panzer-Brigade*, and of the *Schuetzen-Brigade*.

To the above mentioned versions and numbers of *Pz.Bef.Wg. III* produced in the period June 1938-February 1943, it must be recalled that several other tanks were converted to command versions by the *Panzer-Division* maintenance units directly on the field. As we have seen, since the appearance of the *Ausf.J*, the *Pz.Bef.Wg.* were featured by minimum changes from the standard combat tanks, allowing even the units at front to convert standard tanks into command tanks, according to the needs. In this way, many *Pz.Bef.Wg.* were realized from *Pz.Kpfw.III Ausf.J, L,* and *M* chassis, and were successfully operated by their combat units. According to the needs, *Pz.Bef.Wg. III* were also assigned to *Panzer-Artillerie* units, in place of *Pz.Beob. Wg. III*.

In the final years of the war, the main battle tanks of the *Panzerwaffe* were the *Pz.Kpfw.IV* and *V*, and by spring-summer 1944, the *Pz.Kpfw. III* almost disappeared from the front line panzer units. However, the command versions remained in service as long as possible, and – in spite of the heavy losses suffered on all fronts – some of them were still in service in 1945.

Panzer-Beobachtungswagen III (Sd.Kfz.143)

In 1942, together with the planned introduction into service of the new self-propelled guns for the *Panzer-Artillerie Regiment* of the *Panzer-Division* (*le.Feldhaub.18/2 (Sfl) Wespe* and *schw.Feldhaub. 18/1 (Sfl) Hummel*) arose the need to provide those units with a dedicated armoured vehicle for observation, able to provide the artillery forward observation officers with the same mobility and protection of the tanks in the armoured formations, which they had to follow, in order to direct the fire in support of their operations.

It was considered that the best solution was to design a dedicated version of the new *Pz.Kpfw.V Panther*, but since this tank was still in its test and development phase, it was decided to realize an interim solution which could be produced and delivered in short time. Thus, it was decided to re-built old versions of *Pz.Kpfw. III* tank, which were outdated, and available

◀ A Pz.Bef.Wg.III Ausf.J *(but it could be also an Ausf.L or M converted) taken on the eastern front, in spring 1944. Note the* Sternantenne D *on the rear, the lack of the MG in the front plate, and the code "R01" in a light color, probably in yellow. This tank, still wearing a whitewash camo, belonged to the* Stab *of* Pz.Rgt.25, *of* 7. Panzer-Division. (Zellingen via JR)

▼ *A* Pz.Bef.Wg.III Ausf.K *operated by the* Stab *of* Pz.Rgt.2, *of* 16. Panzer-Division, *taken on the eastern front in February 1944. The tank received a complete whitewash camouflage, with the exception of the left front fender, where the* Division, *and the* Pz.Nachr. Abt. *markings were left visible. See profile at page 49.* (Schick via JR)

in large numbers, introducing new features specific for the artillery observation role. The new design was realised by Alkett, and concerned above all the turret. Works included the removal of the 5 cm KwK gun and its 35 mm thick gun mantle, and their replacement with a 50 mm thick gun mantle, equipped with a fake gun tube on the right side, and a machine-gun ball mount in the middle. Observation of the battlefield was granted by the installation inside the turret of a *Turmbeobachtungsfernrohr 2* (TBF.2), with 10x magnification and 5.7° field of view. This optic could be raised and pivoted thanks to a hole cut in the roof of the turret. Inside the turret commander's cupola it could be possible to mount a SF.14Z scissors periscope, and a TRS.1 (with 6x magnification) periscope. The radio equipment of the *Pz.Beob.Wg.III* included one Fu 8 set (used to pass the fire corrections directly to battery, and to each gun, when distances were in the range 5-20 km), one Fu 4 set, one *Funksprechtgeraet f* (*FuSpr.f*, used to pass the fire corrections when distances were no more than 4-5 km), and one *Tornisterfunkgeraet g* (*TornFu.g*) a backpack man portable radio set. To make room for the extra radio equipment, the MG.34 ball mount on the front armour was replaced by a simple pistol port with a plug. This version maintained the 2.0 m pole antenna on the right side of the superstructure, and added a *Sternantenne D* on the rear engine deck, the same equipment used in the *Pz.Bef. Wg.III Ausf.J*. Starting in May-June 1943, also this version of the *Pz.Kpfw.III* was equipped with *Schuerzen* around the turret and on the sides, in order to increase protection. For the same reason, starting in early 1944, as retrofit, some *Pz.Beob.Wg.III* received also a *Zimmerit* coating.

The *Pz.Beob.Wg.III* were produced by the Deutsche Eisenwerke plant in Duisberg, by converting rebuilt samples of *Pz.Kpfw.III*, mostly from *Ausf.F* and *G* chassis. Only some *Pz.Beob. Wg.III* were produced from *Ausf.E, J, L,* and *M* chassis. A total of 262 tanks were transformed, in the period from February 1943 to April 1944. These vehicles were assigned to self-propelled artillery battalions (*Artillerie-Abteilung (Sfl.)* of the *Panzer* units equipped with *Wespe* and *Hummel* self-propelled guns. At the beginning, in January 1943, it was decided that each battery (*Batterie*) equipped with *Wespe* was authorized to receive two *Pz.Beob. Wg.III*, while each battery equipped with *Hummel* had three. In addition, one-two tanks were assigned also to the *Stabsbatterie* of each *Artillerie-Regiment (mot.)*, and two to the *Stabsbatterie* of each self-propelled artillery battalion. In particular, *K.St.N. 577* of 1 November 1943 assigned one *Pz.Beob.Wg. III* to each *Stabsbatterie* of the *Artillerie-Regiment (mot.)* of a *Panzer-Division*; *K.St.N. 407* of 16 January 1943 and K.St.N. 583 of 1 November 1943 assigned two *Pz.Beob.Wg.III* to each *Stabsbatterie (mot.)* of *Artillerie Abteilung (Sfl.)*; K.St.N. 461b of 16 January 1943 assigned three *Pz.Beob. Wg.III* to each *Batterie Schwere Feldhaubitzen 18/1 (Sfl.)* (equipped with Hummel self-propelled guns); K.St.N. 431b of 1 November 1943 assigned two *Pz.Beob.Wg.III* to each *Batterie Leichte Feldhaubitze 18/2 (Sfl.)* (equipped with *Wespe* self-propelled guns).

The first deliveries occurred in preparation of operation "*Zitadelle*", in May 1943, and included the *Panzer-Division* destined to take part to this major offensive. On 1 May 1943, four *Pz.Beob.Wg.III* were received by *9. And 20. Pz.Div.* Before the end of June, other tanks were assigned as follows: ten to *Pz.Gr.Div. "Grossdeutschland"*, nine to *2. and 4. Pz.Div.* and to *SS-Pz. Gr.Div. "LSSAH"* and *"Das Reich"*, four to *11.Pz.Div.*, and two to *3.Pz.Div.* The *Pz.Beob.Wg.III* remained in service until the end of the war. A report of 15 January 1945 confirmed that 58 of these tanks were still in service at that time, and by 15 March 1945 the number was reduced to 31 tanks. ❏

▲ *Interesting color photo of a Pz.Bef. Wg.III Ausf.J code "556" from the Stab of I/SS-Pz.Rgt. "LSSAH" taken just before Operation "Zitadelle", in early July 1943. Note the color scheme, typical of this unit in summer 1943:* Dunkelgelb *oversprayed with patches of* Olivegruen. *(copyright reserved)*

Pz.Bef.Wg. Ausf.D1, code "RN1", Nachrichten-Abteilung 79, **4.Panzer-Division**, Poland, September 1939.

This tank had the standard colour finish of the period, *Dunkelgrau* with 1/3 stripes of *Dunkelbraun*. The markings include the German national *Balkenkreuz* in yellow outlined white, on the turret sides, and rear of the hull. The "RN1" code was in yellow, painted on the turret sides and rear. At the start of the Polish campaign, the crosses were white, but in order to reduce their visibility, they were soon repainted yellow, while the one on the front plate was cancelled.

Befehlspanzer • 33

Pz.Bef.Wg. Ausf.E, no code, Nachr.Abt. 90, **10.Panzer-Division**, Poland, September 1939.

This vehicle was camouflaged in the standard *Dunkelgrau-Dunkelbraun* colour scheme of the period. The only visible markings are the national crosses, in white, on the turret sides and rear of the hull.

Pz.Bef.Wg. Ausf.D1, code "B02", Nachr.Abt. 39, **3.Panzer-Division**, France, May 1940.

Also this tank was painted in the standard *Dunkelgrau-Dunkelbraun* camouflage used until the end of the French campaign. No German national crosses were present on the sides, but only in the middle of the hull rear, outlined white. The code "B02" was painted outlined white, of the turret sides and rear. The B was probably meaning "*Brigade*", when this tank was detached to the Headquarters of *3. Panzer-Brigade*. A small black rhomboid with the same code was fitted to the sides and to the hull rear plate, over the smoke discharger device. The overall look of this tank was very dusty.

Pz.Bef.Wg. Ausf.E, code "0", Stab Pz.Rgt. 1, **1.Panzer-Division**, France, May 1940.

The colour scheme was the standard grey-brown of this period, while the makings included a single digit "0", plus a small dot, both in white on the sides of the turret. On the left side of the gun mantle it was painted the *1.Pz-Div.* badge, while on the front plate there was a squared additional plate showing the German national cross, outlined white. Near the digit "0" it seems that it was fitted a base, possibly for an additional radio antenna.

Pz.Bef.Wg. Ausf.E, code "II01", Stab II/Pz.Rgt.2, **1.Panzer-Division**, Belgium, May 1940.

The colour scheme was the standard grey-brown of the period. Markings included the national German crosses, in black outlined white, on the superstructure sides and hull rear, plus the code "II01" in white, on the turret sides and rear. The white bar under the code was the identification marking of Pz-Rgt.2. On the turret roof there was a white cross, while a white rectangle for aerial recognition was painted on the engine deck. This tank was used by *Hauptmann* Gitterman, the commander of *II Abteilung, Pz-Rgt.2*.

Befehlspanzer • 35

Pz.Bef.Wg. Ausf.E, code "I03", Stab I/Pz.Rgt.11, **6.Panzer-Division**, Holland, May 1940.

The colour scheme of this tank was the *Dunkelgrau* overall, adopted from July 1940. Markings included the national crosses, in black outlined white, on the superstructure sides and hull rear, plus the divisional badge, two crosses in yellow, worn on the turret sides, front plate, and rear hull. The code "I03", assigned to the third command tank of the radio platoon in the battalion HQ, was in white.

Pz.Bef.Wg. Ausf.H, code "B", Nachr.Abt. 90, **10.Panzer-Division**, Germany, March 1941.

This model already had the new drive sprocket wheel, but maintained the old idler wheel. Camouflage was overall *Dunkelgrau*. The code "B" was white outlined on the turret sides, while rhomboid plates showed the full code "B01" assigned to this tank, that probably was operated by the *Stab* of *4. Panzer-Brigade*. The German crosses were black outlined white.

Pz.Bef.Wg. Ausf.H, code "D02", Nachr.Abt. 89, **11.Panzer-Division**, Yugoslavia, April 1941.

This tank was painted in the standard *Dunkelgrau* colour scheme. Markings included the German national cross, in black and white on the superstructure sides and rear, and the standard Divisional insignia, in yellow, on the front part of the superstructure. The code was "D02", in white, on the turret sides. Its meaning was probably "*Division*", this being a command tank detached to the *Division Stab*. This was an early Ausf.H, which maintained the fake gun, drive sprocket and idler wheels of the *Ausf.E* model.

Pz.Bef.Wg. Ausf.H, code "III01", Stab III/Pz.Rgt.25, **7.Panzer-Division**, Russia, July 1941.

This tank appeared to be painted in *Dunkelgrau* overall, and received also a sprocket wheel of the new type. Markings included the code "III01", in red outlined white, in the three usual positions on the turret, plus the German crosses in black and white, on the superstructure sides, and rear plate. The divisional badge, in yellow, was painted on the front plate, left of the driver's visor. Note the large wooden beam carried on the left side, to help when crossing rough terrain.

Befehlspanzer • 37

Pz.Bef.Wg. Ausf.H, code "R01", Stab Pz.Rgt.5, **21.Panzer-Division**, Libya, summer 1941.

This early model *Ausf.H* showed a single camouflage paint, based on the *RAL 8000 Gelbbraun* colour. On the turret sides there was the code "R01" in white outline, and the German crosses were in white outline too. On the front plate it sported the standard Division marking together with the *Afrika Korps* palm, which was repeated also on the sides of the stowage box on the rear.

Pz.Bef.Wg. Ausf.H, code "30", Stab Pz.Rgt.18, **18.Panzer-Division**, Russia, summer 1941.

This command version was modified as *Tauchpanzer*, for amphibious operations. The overall colour scheme was *Dunkelgrau*. Markings included the Regimental badge, in black and white, on the turret sides, together with the division marking, in yellow, and to the individual code "30" in white. A large stowage box was carried on the rear engine deck.

Pz.Bef.Wg. Ausf.H, code "R", Stab Pz.Rgt.8, **15.Panzer-Division**, Libya, autumn 1941.

This tank appeared to be painted in *Gelbbraun RAL 8000* overall, with a heavy layer of dust and sand. On the turret sides it wore the code "R" in red, as *Pz-Rgt.8* didn't use platoon and tank numbers in its codes. In the middle of the front plate there was the white palm, badge of the *Afrika Korps*. The pole antenna on the right side had the *Division Stab* pennant, while a large stowage box was fitted on the engine deck. This was an early model *Bef.Pz.Wg. Ausf.H*.

Pz.Bef.Wg. Ausf.H, code "I00", Stab SS-Pz. Abt."Wiking", **SS-Division (mot.) "Wiking"**, Russia, early May 1942.

This late *Ausf.H* was painted in *Dunkelgrau* overall, while the markings included the code "I00" in white outline, on the turret sides, plus the German crosses, in black and white, on the superstructure sides, and rear plate. The division badge, in white over a black circle, was painted on the right front fender.

Befehlspanzer • 39

Pz.Bef.Wg. Ausf.H, code "IN1", Stab I/Pz.Rgt.36, **14.Panzer-Division**, Russia, summer 1942.

The colour scheme was *Dunkelgrau*, and the markings included the code "IN1" in yellow, on the turret sides and rear, plus the division badge in yellow, on the turret sides. Note the sprocket and idler wheels of the new type, and the big stowage box on the rear engine deck.

Pz.Bef.Wg. Ausf.H, code "372", Stab. Pz.Rgt.24, **24.Panzer-Division**, Russia, summer 1942.

Also this tank was in the standard *Dunkelgrau* camouflage, with no additional colours. Markings included the code "372" in white, on the turret sides and on the rear stowage box, plus the division badge in white on the right end of the rear plate, near the German cross, in white outline. The German crosses in white outline were painted also on the superstructure sides. A small white rectangle was painted on the gun tube. Note the late model sprocket and idler wheels, and the new 5 cm-like fake gun, which replaced the old 3.7cm.

40 • Befehlspanzer

Pz.Bef.Wg. Ausf.H, code "405", Stab SS-Pz. Abt."LSSAH", **SS-Division (mot.) Leibstandarte SS Adolf Hitler ("LSSAH")**, France, July 1942.

This tank was in the standard *Dunkelgrau* overall, and included the code "405" in white outlined on the turret sides and rear. The German crosses were black and white, on the superstructure sides, and on the rear plate, while the divisional marking was on the right side of the rear plate, and probably on the left side of the front plate. At that time, *SS-Pz-Abt.1* had only three companies, while the *Stab* had tanks in the "400" series.

Pz.Bef.Wg. Ausf.K, code "01", Stab Pz.Rgt. "Grossdeutschland", **Infanterie-Division (mot.) "Grossdeutschland"**, Ukraine, February 1943.

This tank was finished in *Dunkelgrau*, but in spite of the snow covered land in Ukraine in February, it was not whitewashed. Markings included the code "01" in white outline, in the three usual positions on the turret, plus the German crosses, on the superstructure sides, and rear plate. Under the code, a square in a light colour (probably yellow) was painted. The *Ausf.K* was the final development of the *Befehlspanzer* on Pz.III chassis, and it was armed with the 5 cm KwK.39 (L/60) gun.

Pz.Bef.Wg. Ausf.J, code "I01", Stab I/SS-Pz. Rgt."Totenkopf", **SS-Panzer-Grenadier-Division "Totenkopf"**, Ukraine, February 1943.

This tank had a *Dunkelgrau* overall finish, covered with a seasonal whitewash, except for the front sides of the turret, in order to make visible the code "I01", in white outlined black.

The German crosses were black and white, in the three standard positions, while the division badge was painted in white, on the front plate near the driver's visor.

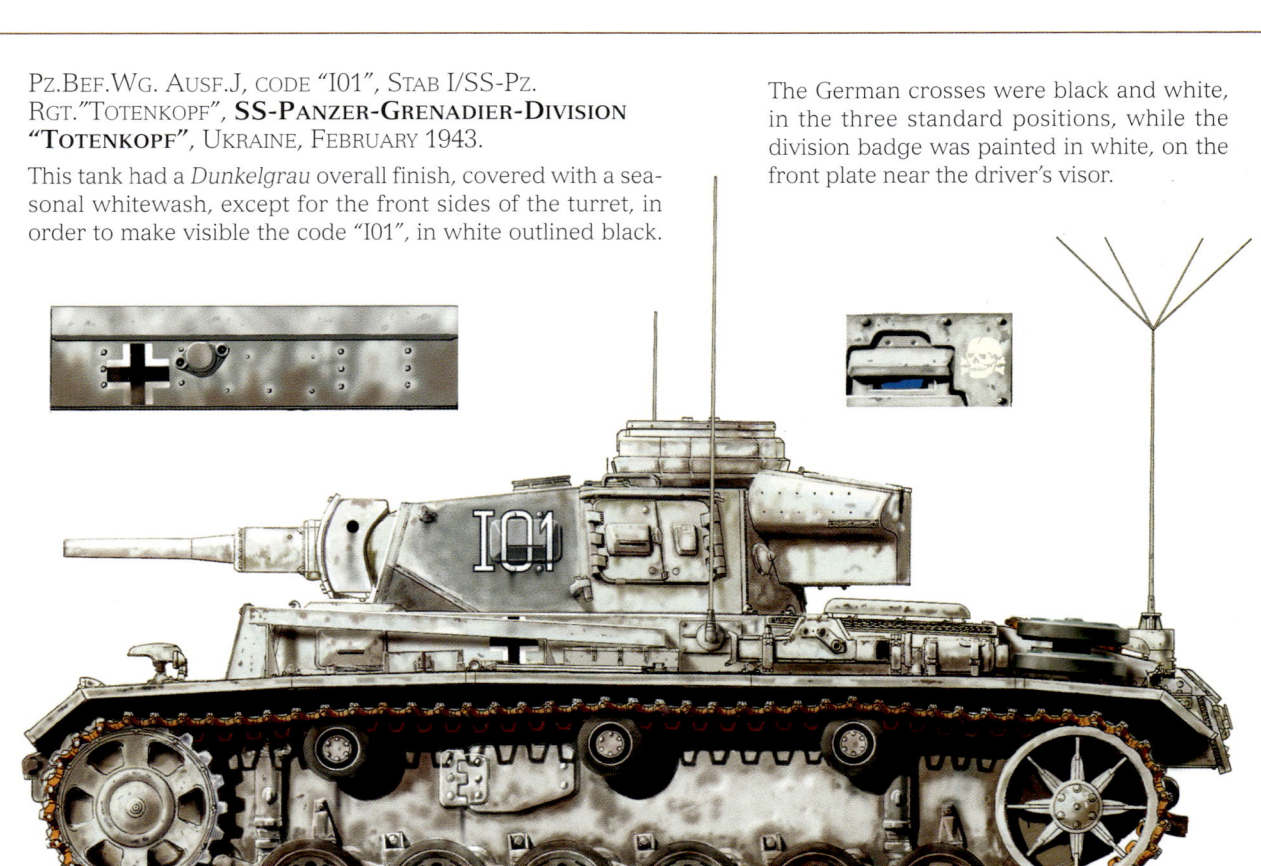

Pz.Bef.Wg. Ausf.J, code "555", Stab II/SS-Pz. Rgt."LSSAH", **SS-Panzer-Grenadier-Division "LSSAH"**, Ukraine, March 1943.

This tank was completed in the standard *Dunkelgrau*, but for winter operations at Kharkov received a whitewash. Only the rear side of the *Rommelkiste* was left with no white paint, showing the shape of the code numbers, in white outline. On the turret sides, the code left visible was only the grey part inside the white outline. The German crosses were black and white on the three standard positions, while that on the back appeared to be only black, probably due to dirt. On the front plate, there was the division badge, in white.

The Ausf.J was the first version to adopt the *Sternantenne D* in place of the frame antenna on the engine deck. It was also the first to receive a traversable turret, armed with a real 5 cm Kw.K. (L/42) gun.

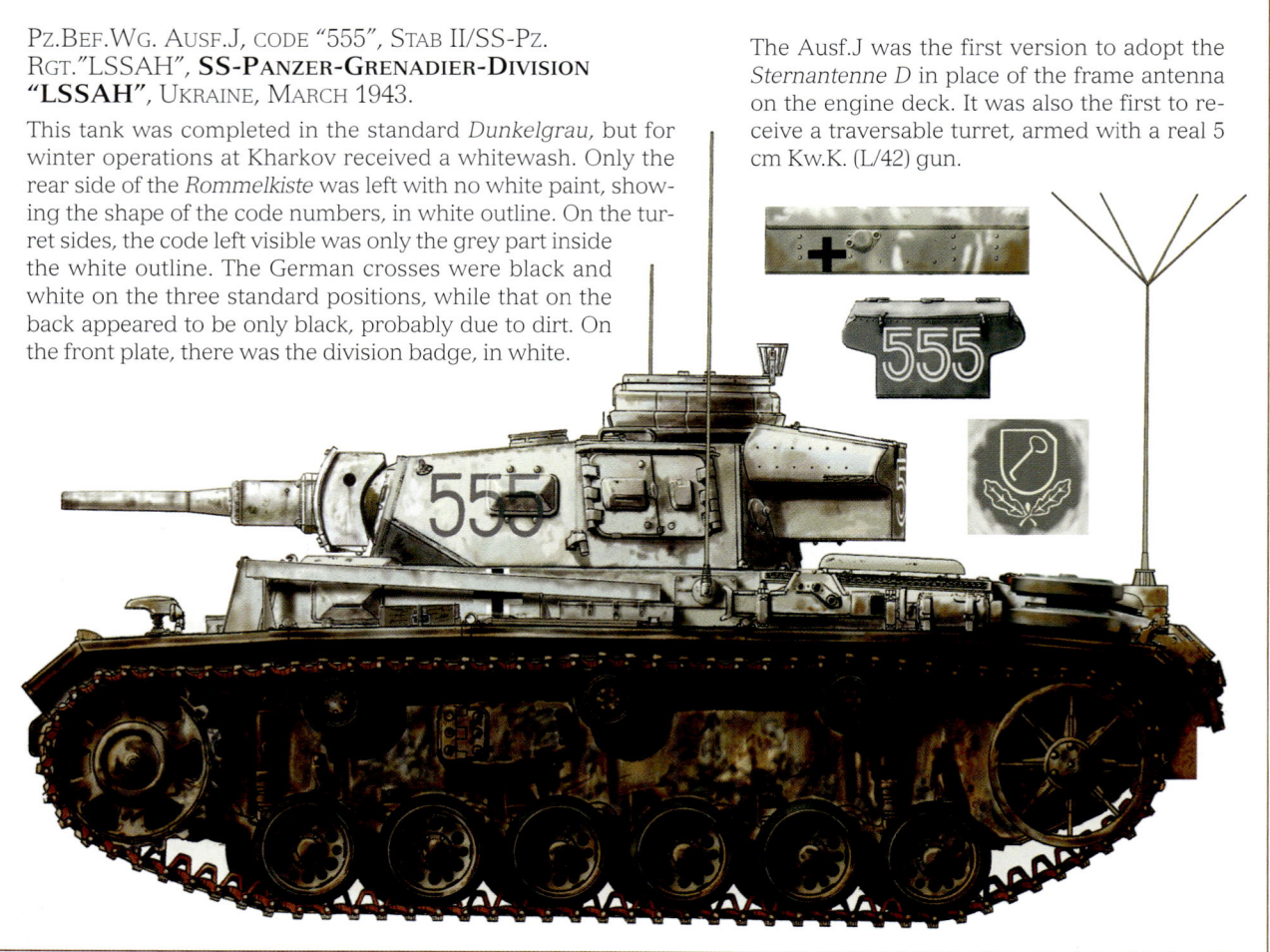

42 • *Befehlspanzer*

Pz.Bef.Wg. Ausf.H, code "D01", Nachrichten-Abteilung 79, **4.Panzer-Division**, Russia, March 1943.

This early *Ausf.H* was still painted in the original *Dunkelgrau* colour scheme, with a typical winter whitewash. The only visible marking is the code "D01" (D probably indicating the *Division Stab*) in yellow, on the two sides of the turret. A large stowage box was fitted to the rear engine deck.

Panzer-Beobachtungswagen III Ausf.G, Pz.Art. Rgt.102, **9.Panzer-Division**, Ukraine, May 1943.

This was one of the first *Pz.Beob.Wg. III* delivered to the front, in preparation of operation "*Zitadelle*". It was brand new, finished in the factory standard *Dunkelgelb*, and the only markings were the German national crosses, in black and white.

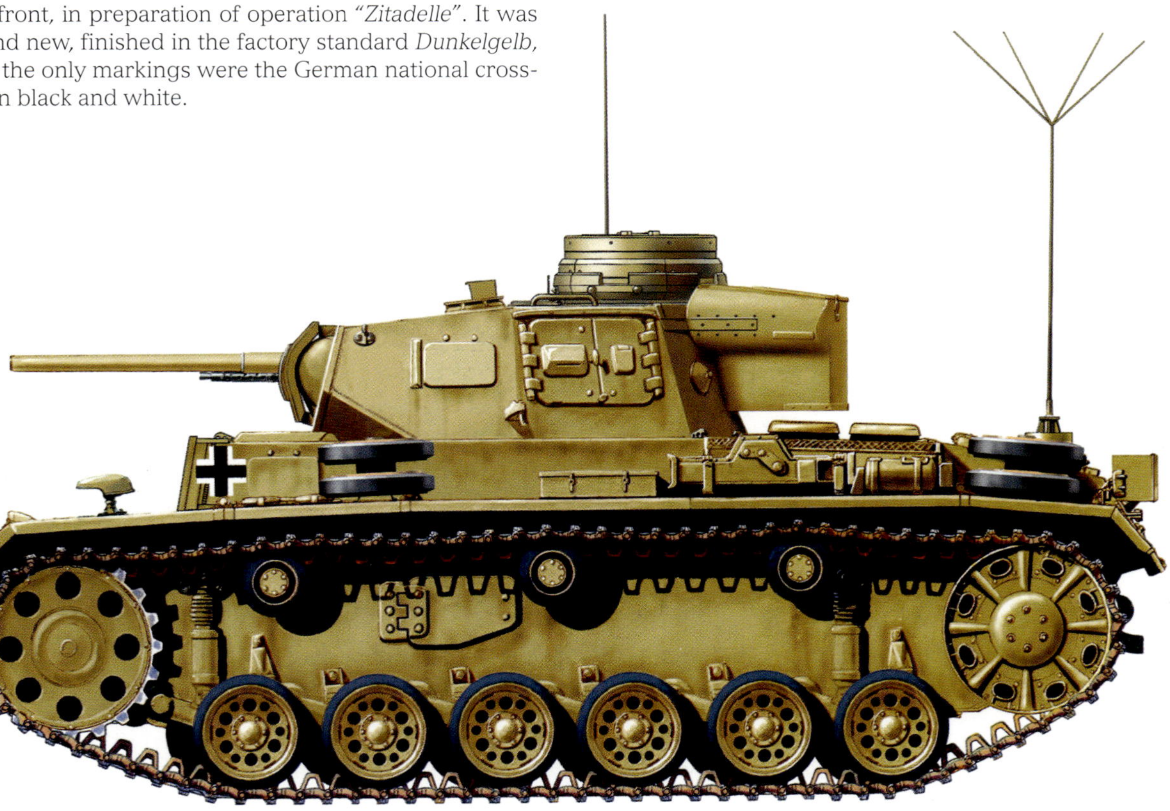

Pz.Beob.Wg. III Ausf.G, code "A1", Pz.Art.Rgt. "Grossdeutschland", **Panzer-Grenadier-Division "Grossdeutschland"**, Ukraine, June 1943.

Following the divisional standard finish in summer 1943, also this tank had a camouflage scheme made of *Olivergrun* lightly sprayed on the basic *Dunkelgelb*. Markings included the code "A1" in white outline, on the three positions on the turret *Schuerzen*, plus the national crosses, in white outline too, on the side *Schuerzen*, and on the rear plate. In this profile it's possible to see the TRS.1 observation periscope, in raised position from the commander's cupola.

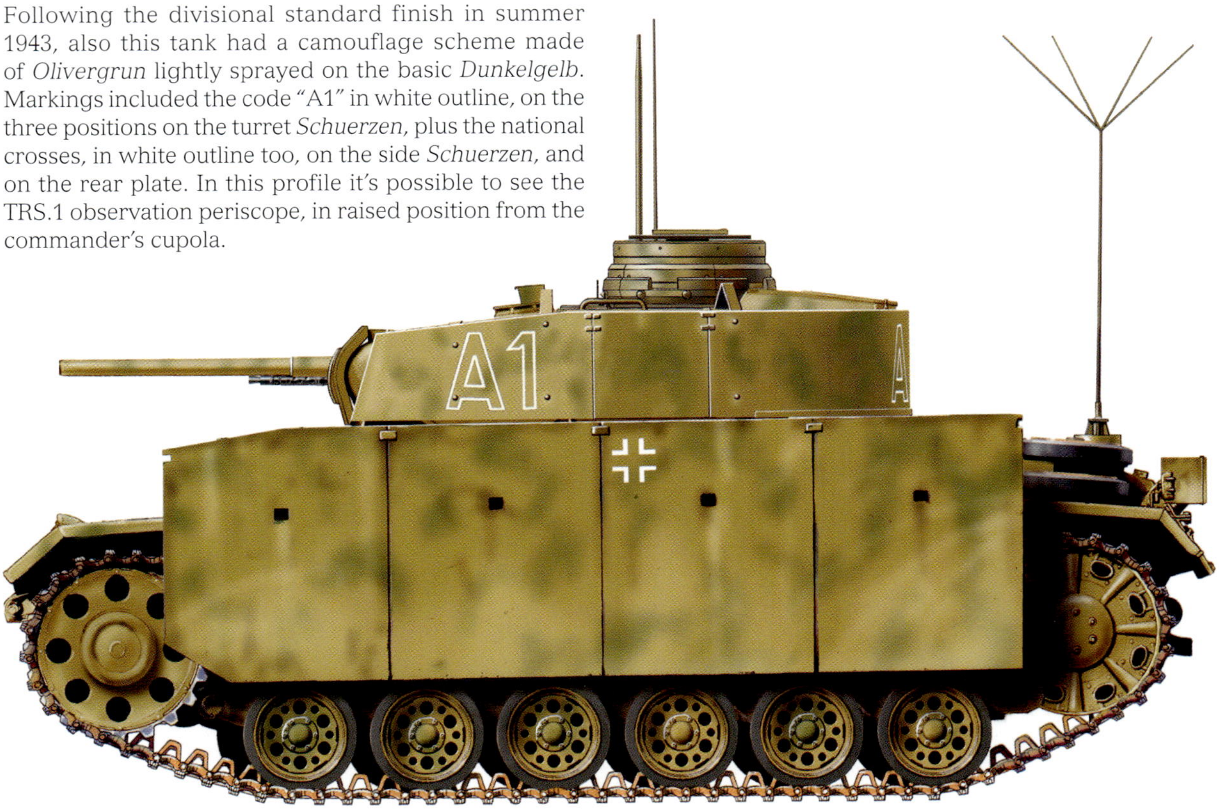

Pz.Bef.Wg. Ausf.H, code "R01", Stab Pz.Rgt.15, **11.Panzer-Division**, Ukraine, July 1943.

This was a late *Ausf.H*, featured by the 5 cm fake gun and by the new type idler wheel (but with an old sprocket wheel), and re-equipped in June with the new spaced armour, the *Schuerzen*. The camouflage is formed by *Dunkelgelb* oversprayed with *Olivgruen* mottle, re-painted over the original *Dunkelgrau*. The markings include the "R01" in black, on the three positions on the turret *Schuerzen*, plus the division mark (special version for operation "Zitadelle") in black on the rear plate, and probably on the superstructure sides. The German crosses were black and white. Note the two steps opened on the side *Schuerzen*, to ease the climbing on the tank.

Pz.Bef.Wg. Ausf.J, code "R2", Stab SS-Pz. Rgt."DR", **SS-Panzer-Grenadier-Division "Das Reich"**, Ukraine, July 1943.

This tank received the camouflage which became standard after spring 1943, a base of *Dunkelgelb* with the other two colours used to disrupt the shape according to the season, and to the unit orders. The markings included the code "R2", in white outline, on the turret sides and rear, the latter being very roughly handpainted. German crosses were white outline, on the superstructure sides and rear, while the division special badge for operation "*Zitadelle*" was painted in white, on the front plate. Note that this tank had two 2 m antennas on the sides, plus an unusually long (about 2.7 m) pole antenna on the engine deck, this probably meaning that it was an SdKfz.268 (*Flivo*) version.

Pz.Bef.Wg. Ausf.J, code "926", Stab Pz.Rgt.201, **23.Panzer-Division**, Ukraine, July 1943.

This tank was camouflaged with the standard two colours of the period, oversprayed on the factory finish of *Dunkelgelb*. Markings included the code "926" in black outlined white, in the three standard positions on the turret *Schuerzen*, plus the national crosses, in black and white, on the side *Schuerzen*, and on the rear plate. No divisional markings were visible. The staff unit adopted a code in the "900" series, as no 9th Company existed in *Pz-Rgt.201*.

Befehlspanzer • 45

Pz.Bef.Wg. Ausf.K, code "0", Stab Pz.Rgt. "Grossdeutschland, **Panzer-Grenadier-Division "Grossedeutschland"**, Ukraine, July 1943.

This tank was finished in *Dunkelgelb*, with a light mottled overspray of *Olivgruen*. Markings included the code "0", in white outline, on the three usual positions on the turret *Schuerzen*, plus the national crosses, on the side *Schuerzen*, and on the rear plate, in white outline. No divisional badge was present.

BefehlsPz.Kpfw.III Ausf.L, code "I02", Stab I/Pz.Rgt.25, **7. Panzer-Division**, Ukraine, July 1943.

Similarly to many tanks which fought in summer 1943, also in operation "*Zitadelle*", this was finished in *Dunkelgelb*, with a light overspray in *Olivgruen*. Markings included the code "I02" in black outlined white, on the turret *Schurzen* sides, plus the special divisional badge for "*Zitadelle*", in black, near the driver's visor. Note that this tank was a standard *Ausf.L* converted on the field to the command role.

Pz.Beob.Wg. III Ausf.G, code "A04", Pz.Art.Rgt. 102, **9.Panzer-Division**, Ukraine, July 1943.

This tank was upgraded in June with the new *Schuerzen*, and received a light camouflage of *Olivgruen* and *Schokobraun* oversprayed lines. The only apparent marking is the code "A04" ("A" meaning *Artillerie*) in black, on the three usual positions on the turret *Schuerzen*. Probably, it also has a black and white German cross on the rear plate.

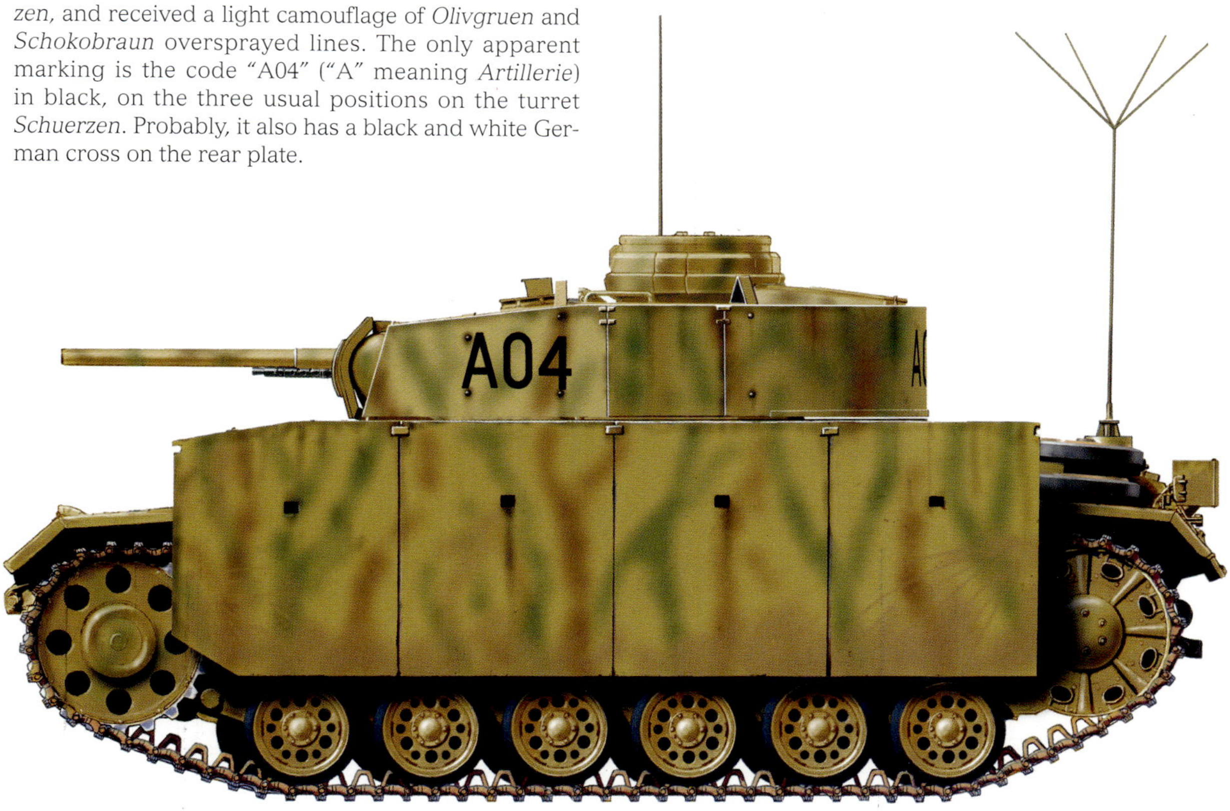

Pz.Beob.Wg. III Ausf.G, code "B51", SS-Art.Rgt. "LSSAH", **SS-Panzer-Grenadier-Division "LSSAH"**, Ukraine, July 1943.

This tank had a basic colour of *Dunkelgelb* overall, oversprayed with waves of *Olivgruen*. Markings included the code "B51" (hand painted) in black outlined white, on the turret *Schuerzen* sides, plus the national crosses, in black and white, on the side *Schuerzen*, and probably on the rear plate.

Befehlspanzer • 47

Pz.Beob.Wg. III Ausf.G, code "?51", II/Pz.Art. Rgt.16, **16.Panzer-Division**, Italy, September 1943.

This tank had as only camouflage its basic coat of *Dunkelgelb*, received at the factory. The markings include the code "51" in black outline, on the three usual positions of the turret *Schuerzen*. On the rear sides of the turret *Schuerzen* there were also the German national crosses, in black and white. Is it possible that the full code of this tank was "A51" or "B51", but in the available photos the left part of the rear turret *Schuerzen* is missing.

Pz.Bef.Wg. Ausf.H, code "IN2", Stab I/Pz.Rgt.31, **5.Panzer-Division**, Russia, late 1943.

This early *Ausf.H* (but equipped with turret *Schuertzen*, and with a late idler wheel) had the basic Dunkelgrau re-painted with the *Dunkelgelb* colour. The markings include the code "IN2" in yellow, on the turret *Schuertzen*, coupled to the *Pz-Rgt.31* badge, a red devil's head. Also this tank was equipped with a large stowage box on the engine deck.

48 • Befehlspanzer

Pz.Bef.Wg. Ausf.H, Stab Pz.Rgt. 35, **4.Panzer-Division**, Russia, late 1943.

This tank received the new colour scheme adopted in February 1943, formed by a basis of *Dunkelgelb*, oversprayed (when decided by the personnel) with *Olivegruen* and *Schokobraun*, all whitewashed due to the snow environment. The markings included a standing bear (in green, colour of the *Stab*), plus the *4.Pz-Div.* badge, in black and yellow, and the nickname *"Baerenfuehrer"* (chief of the bears), all on the turret sides. Note the presence of a new sprocket wheel, and of an old idler wheel.

Pz.Bef.Wg. Ausf.K, Nachrichten-Abteilung 16, **16.Panzer-Division**, Russia, winter 1944.

This tank received a very neat whitewash over the basic *Dunkelgelb* finish. The only visible markings were the divisional badge, in yellow, and the *Nachrichten-Abt.* Tactical sign, in white, both painted on the left front fender, which was left with no whitewash paint. No codes on the turret.

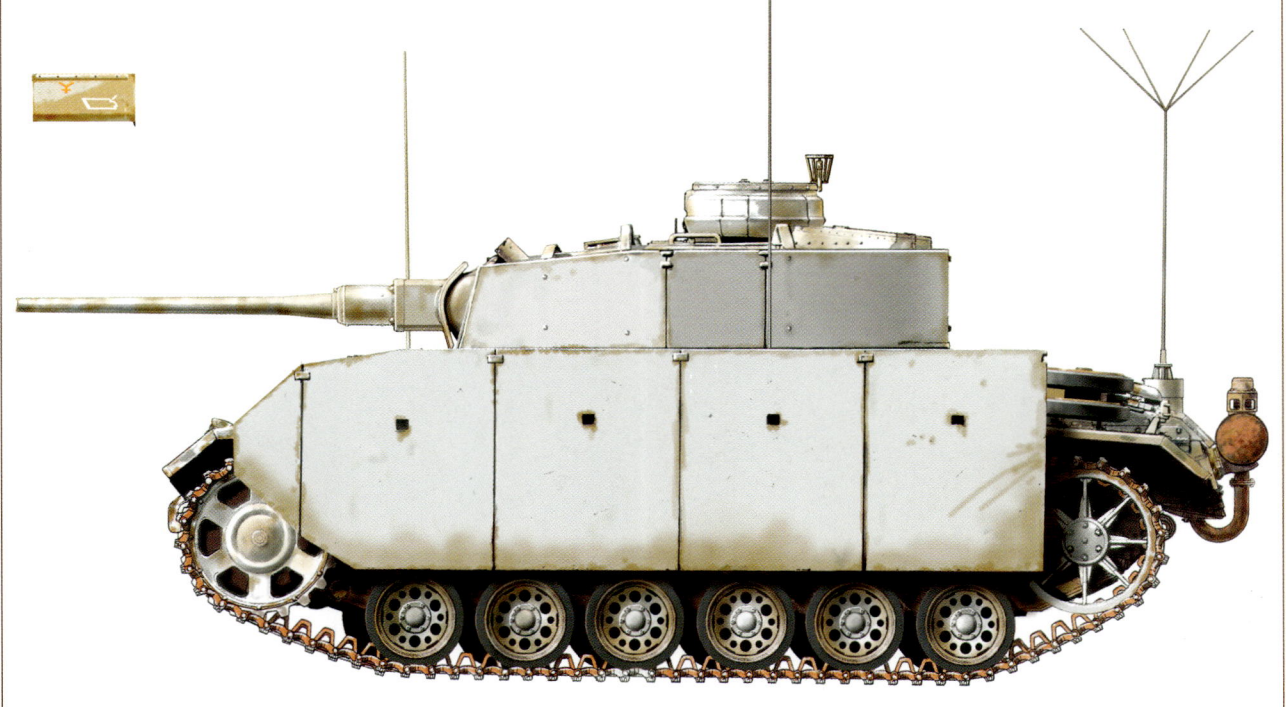

Befehlspanzer • 49

Pz.Bef.Wg. Ausf.J, code "II", probably Stab Pz.Abt.5, **25. Panzer-Grenadier-Division**, Russia, spring 1944.

This tank was camouflaged with the only *Dunkelgelb* finish, and the markings included the code "II" in red outlined white (probably meaning that this was the second tank of the Stab), on the turret *Schuerzen* in the three usual positions, plus the national crosses, in black and white, on the side *Schuerzen* and on the rear plate. Note the presence of an old sprocket wheel, and the AA MG mount on the commander's cupola.

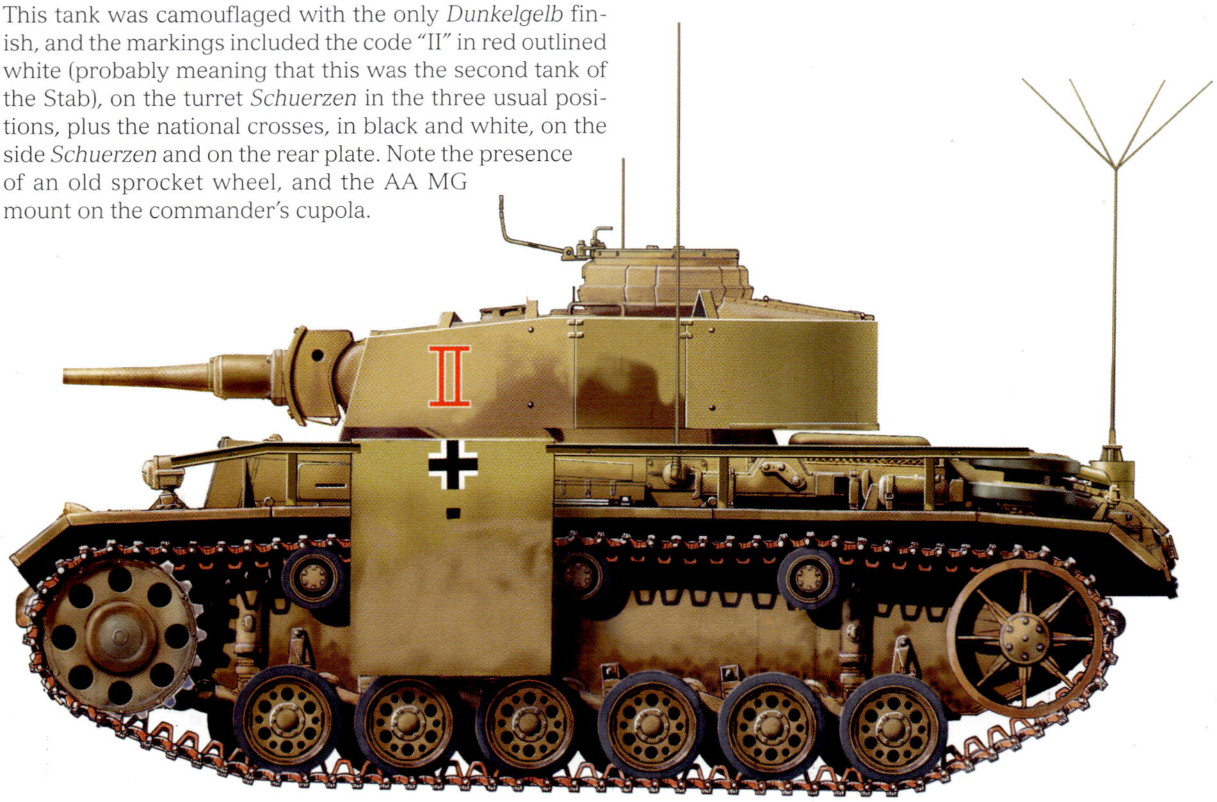

BefehlsPz.Kpfw. III Ausf.L, code "001", Pz.Art.Rgt. 103, **4.Panzer-Division**, Latvia, September 1944.

This was a standard *Pz.Kpfw. III Ausf.L* converted on the field to be operated as a command/observation tank by *Panzer-Artillerie-Rgt. 103*, and was equipped with a *Sternantenne D*, fitted to the right fender. The camouflage consisted in a mix of the three standard colours, and probably some parts of this tank where repainted. Markings included the code "001", in black outlined white, on the two rear sides of the turret *Schuerzen*, while on the front sides there were the German crosses, in black and white outlined. On the front left turret *Schuerzen* it was painted the name "Brigitte". Note the early model sprocket wheel

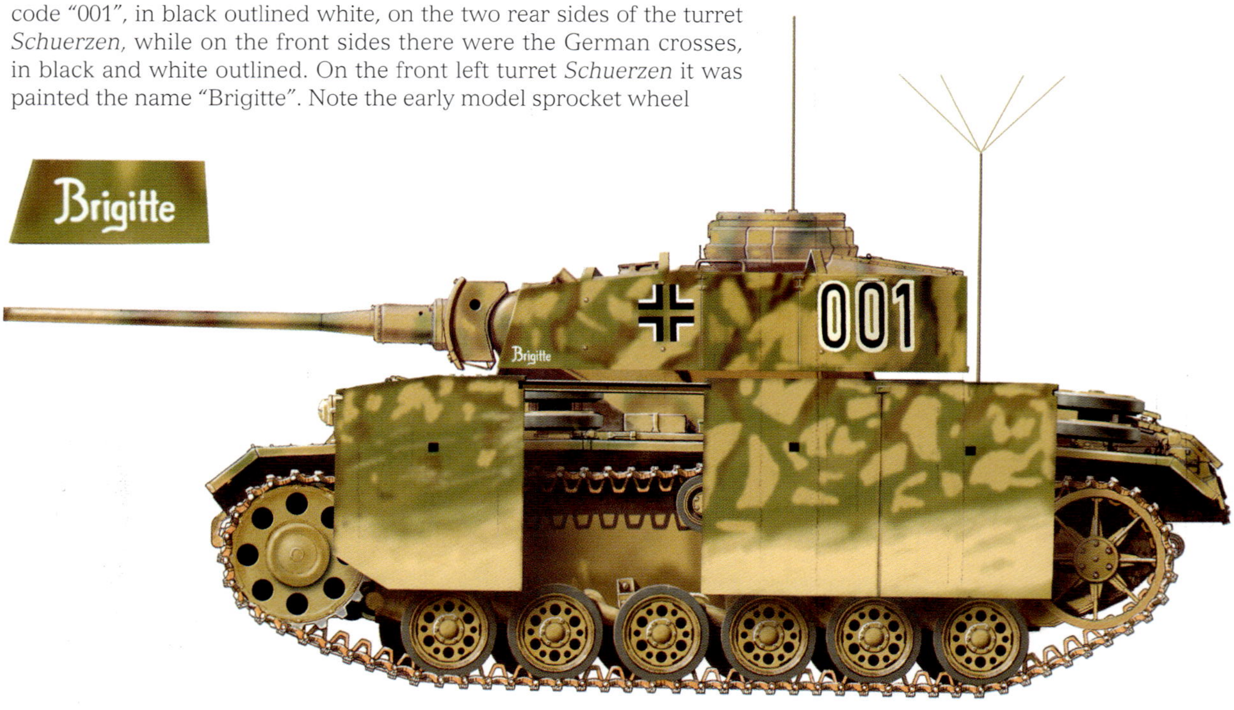

Pz.Kpfw.IV chassis

PANZER-BEFEHLSWAGEN IV

As the war progressed, the *Panzerwaffe* gradually and constantly tried to improve its combat capabilities with the development, production and introduction into service of better tanks. At the same time, older models and variants, which were becoming outdated, were gradually disappearing from the combat units, due to losses from the enemy, as well as retirement and re-assignment to secondary roles and training duties.

That was the case also for the *Pz.Kpfw.III*, and part of its versions, which by early 1943 were already outclassed by the new American and above all Russian tanks. Even if the *Pz.Bef.Wg.III* were still available in good numbers, in the second half of 1943 it was considered that a new type of command tank had to be developed, this being on the *Pz.Kpfw.IV* chassis, in order to better integrate (an conceal) it in the front line *Panzer-Regiment*.

As early as 1942, some combat units had already started to convert *Pz.Kpfw.IV* standard tanks to the command role, thanks to modification works carried out by the field maintenance units. Photo evidences exist of a *Pz.Kpw.IV Ausf.F1* from *20.Pz.Div.* which was field modified with a frame antenna on the engine deck, possibly using components of other wrecked command vehicles. The same unit operated a *Pz.Kpw.IV Ausf.G*, upgraded with *Schuerzen*, with a similar frame antenna mount during the battle of Kursk, in July 1943. Such conversions from standard combat tanks (mainly *Ausf.G*) were made easier when the equipment for the command role was simplified, and the *Sternantenne D* set became available.

However, official decisions about the realization of *Pz.Bef.Wg.IV* produced by the industry in Germany became real only at the beginning of 1944. In March of that year, in fact, it was decided to start the conversion of rebuild *Pz.Kpfw.IV* (*Ausf.H* and *J*) to the new command standard. This was much simplified compared to the older *Pz.Bef.Wg.III* types, and basically consisted in the integration of a new set of radios and associated antennas. Works were assigned to Nibelungwerke.

The *Sd.Kfz.267* version received a Fu 8 radio set, and a Fu 5 radio set. The first was associated to a *Sternantenne D*, mounted on a base covered with a porcelain insulator protected by an armoured guard, fitted on the rear right

▶ *Some* Pz.Kpfw.IV *and* Sd.Kfz.251 *from* 7. Panzer-Division *taken in Kurland, in October 1944. The tank in the foreground is a* Pz.Bef.Wg.IV, *as it is equipped with a* Sternantenne D *on the rear right side, plus a 2 m pole antenna on the rear left side.* (Ulrich via JR)

▲ *A* Pz.Bef.Wg.IV Ausf.H *from the* Stab *of* II/SS-Pz.Rgt.12 *taken near Rouen, France, in May 1944. Note the lack of markings, with the exception of the Division badge, on the right front fender, and the presence of only one antenna, a* Sternantenne D, *on the rear left side. See profile at page 55.* (BA-101I-493-3355-10-Siedel)

end of the engine deck. The Fu 5 was associated to a 2.0 m pole antenna, mounted on a flexible base on the right side of the turret roof, in place of the *Nahverteidigungswaffe* (close defence weapon). The *Sd.Kfz.268* configuration (destined to ground-air communications) included an Fu 7 radio set, associated to a 1.4 m pole antenna, fitted to the *Pz.Kpfw.IV Ausf.H* standard position, on the rear left side of the engine deck, and an Fu 5, with the antenna again on the turret roof. To provide power to the radio sets, a GG400 auxiliary electric generator was fitted to the rear left end of the fighting compartment. In the *Pz.Bef.Wg.IV* of new production (as for the *Pz.Beob.Wg.IV*), inside the commander's cupola it was fitted the mount for a SF.14Z scissors periscope, which could be used only with the cupola hatch open, while on the front left side of the cupola, a hole was cut to allow the use of a TSR.1 retractable and pivotable periscope. To make room to the additional radio sets, the coaxial MG mount inside the turret was removed. The presence inside the tank of the radios and generator sets, forced to reduce the number of rounds for the 7.5 cm KwK 40 L/48 gun from 87 to 72. The crew consisted of five members, like the standard tanks, but the loader acted also as second radio operator.

From March to July 1944, a total of 88 *Pz.Bef.Wg.IV* were produced thanks to rebuild and conversion works. The only *Pz.Bef.Wg.IV* of new production were 17 tanks which were completed in August and September 1944, on the basis of the *Ausf.J* chassis. Other samples were completed by the maintenance units of the *Panzer-Divisions*, thanks to conversion (sometimes non-standard) of normal combat tanks. Since April 1944, the *Pz.Bef.Wg.IV* were progressively assigned to the *Panzer-Abteilung* equipped with *Pz.Kpfw.IV*, and remained in service until the end of the war. According to *K.St.N. 1150 (fG)* of 1 April 1944, three *Pz.Bef.Wg.IV* had to be assigned to each *Nachrichten und Aufklaerungs Zug* of the *Panzer-Abteilung (freie Gliederung)*, and this was confirmed by *K.St.N. 1107 (fG) Ausf.B* of *1 November 1944*. Finally, *K.St.N. 1107 (fG)* of 1 April 1945 reduced to only two the *Pz.Bef.Wg.IV* destined to the *Nachr.Zug.* of a *Panzer-Abteilung "IV" (freie Gliederung)*.

PANZER-BEOBACHTUNGSWAGEN IV (7.5 CM) AUSF.J

After the completion of the 262 samples of *Pz.Beob.Wg.III* it was decided to fulfil the needs for more artillery observation tanks with the design of a new vehicle, based on a type of tank still in front line use by the *Panzer-Division*.

◀ *The rear view of* Pz.Bef.Wg.IV Ausf.J Fgst.Nr.92200 *shows the position of the armoured pot on the right side of rear plate, housing the base for the* Sternantenne D. *Note on the base the presence of the* Stuetzkorb, *destined to support the additional 70 cm antenna sections* (Verlaengerungsstab) *for long range communications from static position.* (US NARA)

▲◀ *This photo of the captured* Pz.Bef.Wg.IV Ausf.J, Fgst.Nr.92200, *well shows the positions of the TSR.1 periscope (here raised), and of the 2 meters pole antenna on the turret roof. Note that it also lacked the coaxial MG. See profile at page 58.* (US NARA)

▲▶ *An internal view of the* Pz.Bef.Wg.IV Ausf.J *turret, showing the base of the TSR.1 periscope.* (US NARA)

▶ *This photo shows a Pz.Beob.Wg.IV Ausf.J captured by the Russians in Curland, in February 1945. It belonged to* 14. Panzer-Division. *Note the* Sturmgeschuetz-Kommandantenkuppel *commander's cupola, typical feature of this version. See profile at page 59.* (ASKM via WM)

The German Artillery command wanted to use the new *Pz.Kpfw.V Panther* for this task, but difficulties encountered in the approval of this choice by the *Panzertruppen* general staff forced to switch the attention to another design. Thus, in September 1943 it was planned to use for this task the *Pz.Kpfw. IV*, also in this case using old chassis to be rebuilt and converted into *Pz.Beob. Wg.IV*. However, the feedbacks coming from the front line units about the *Pz.Beob.Wg.III* reported a high number of failures due to the fact that many mechanical component of the rebuilt tanks were old and worn out. For this reason, in January 1944 it was decided to use tanks of new production, and to assign the realisation of the *Pz.Beob. Wg.IV* directly to the assembly lines of the Nibelungenwerk factory. Every 25 new *Pz.Kpfw.IV Ausf.J*, one had to be picked up and completed as *Pz.Beob. Wg.IV*. The hull layout of the new version was identical to that of the *Pz.Bef. Wg.IV*, having a *Sternantenne D* and its mount at the right corner of the rear engine deck, while at the left corner side of the engine deck remained the 2.0 m pole antenna of the combat version. The observation version had its main features in the turret. The commander's cupola was replaced by a shorter *Sturmgeschuetz-Kommandantenkuppel*, equipped with seven periscopes, the same cupola adopted on the *Sturmgeschuetz III* and *IV* assault guns. Through a flap in the front of the hatch, the commander could raise a SF.14Z scissors periscope maintaining the hatch closed. The tank was equipped also with a TSR.1 observation periscope, which could be raised and pivoted thanks to a small hatch in the left side of the turret roof. To make room to the extra radio sets, also in this tank the MG mount in the turret was removed. On the right side of the turret, near the *Nahverteidigungswaffe* (close defence weapon), there was the mount for another 2.0 or 1.4 m pole antenna. The communication equipment included one Fu 8 radio set, one Fu 4 radio set, and one *Funksprechgeraet f* set. The necessary power to operate the radios was provided by a GG400 electrical generator, installed in the left rear corner of the combat compartment. As for the *Pz.Bef.Wg.IV*, The presence of the generator and of the radio sets forced to reduce the ammunition rounds carried for the main armament, the 7.5 cm KwK.40 L/48 gun, from 87 to 72 rounds.

Production of the *Pz.Beob.Wg.IV* started in April 1944 (with the first 10 samples completed), and ended in February 1945, after a total production of 203 tanks. The first seven vehicles were accepted in July 1944, and the last 15 in March 1945, for a total of 133 *Pz.Beob. Wg.IV* accepted by the Waffenamt for service. Since 1 May 1944, it was established that only one *Pz.Beob.Wg.* had to be assigned to each self-propelled gun battery. The first *Pz.Beob.Wg.IV* were delivered to the combat units in time to take part to operation "Wacht am Rhein", in December 1944. They were assigned in number of five each to *1.SS, 2.SS, 10.SS, 12.SS-Pz.Div., Pz.Lehr.Div.*, and *Fuehrer-Grenadier-Brigade*; and in number of four to *2. Pz.Div.* On 15 December 1944 other tanks were shipped to *9., 21.,* and *116.Pz.Div.*, too late to be employed in the so called "Battle of the Bulge". In 1945, the rest of the *Pz.Beob. Wg.IV* produced were assigned to *1., 4., 5., 6., 7., 8., 12., 13., 14., 17., 19., 20., 23., 24., 25.,* and *3.SS-Pz.Div.*, and were operated until the very end of the war. ❑

Pz.Bef.Wg.IV (Sd.Kfz.267 and 268) Ausf. J : specifications	
Length:	7.02 m
Width:	2.88 m
Height:	2.68 m
Weight (combat):	25? t
Engine:	Maybach HL120TRM V12 Water-cooled 11.9 lt gasoline, delivering 300 HP at 3,000 rpm
Fuel capacity:	680 lt
Transmission:	ZF SSG 77, with 1 reverse and 6 forward gear
Max speed:	38 km/h
Range (on road):	320 km
Range (cross country):	210 km
Grade:	?°
Trench crossing:	? m
Step:	? cm
Fording depth:	80 cm
Ground clearance:	40 cm
Ground pressure:	0.89 kg/cm2
Power ratio:	12 HP/ton
Weapons:	1 x 7.5 cm Kw.K 40 (L/48) 2 x 7.92mm MG.34 machine gun
Ammunition:	72 (gun)
Protection:	hull front: 80 mm turret front: 50 mm
Communications:	1 x Fu 5, 1 x Fu 8 (SdKfz.267), 1 x Fu 5, 1 x Fu 7 (SdKfz.268)
Crew:	5

BefehlsPz.Kpfw. IV Ausf.F1, code "D04", Nachr.Abt. 92, **20. Panzer-Division**, Russia, summer 1942.

This command tank was realised thanks to a field modification of a standard *Pz.Kpw.IV Ausf.F1*, thanks to the introduction of a *Rahmenantenne* (frame antenna) on the engine deck, destined to a Fu 8 radio set. The overall finish was *Dunkelgrau*, while the markings included the code "D04" in white outline, on the turret sides and rear, plus the division badge, in yellow, on the front part of the turret sides. The German crosses were black and white.

BefehlsPz.Kpfw. IV Ausf.G, code "055", Stab SS-Pz.Rgt.1, **SS-Panzer-Grenadier-Division "LSSAH"**, Ukraine, July 1943.

Also this tank was a field modification of a standard combat tank. It received a second 2 m pole antenna (probably for an Fu 7 radio set) fitted on the rear right side of the turret, near the *Rommelkiste,* inside the turret *Schuerzen*. A periscope sight appeared to come out from the commander's cupola. The tank had the standard *Dunkelgelb* finish, oversprayed with *Olivgruen* patches. Markings included the code "055" in black/white outline on the sides and rear of the turret *Schuerzen* , plus the national crosses, in white outline, on the side *Schuerzen* and on the left side of the rear plate.

54 • *Befehlspanzer*

BefehlsPz.Kpw. IV Ausf.G, code "I", Stab I/Pz.Rgt.21, **20.Panzer-Division**, Ukraine, summer 1943.

This was another field modification performed by the *20.Pz.Div.*, in order to have a combat capable command tank. The standard tank received a frame antenna on the engine deck, which was quite probably associated to a Fu 7 or Fu 8 radio set. The camouflage consisted in a broad *Olivgruen* mottle oversprayed on the basic *Dunkelgelb*. Markings included the "I" code, in white outline, on the sides and rear of turret *Schuerzen*, plus the *Regiment* badge, a white elephant, on the rear left side of the turret *Schuerzen*. The *Division* marking, in yellow on a dark green or dark grey base, was painted on the front plate, near the driver's visor.

Pz.Bef.Wg. IV Ausf.H, Stab II/SS-Pz.Rgt.12, **12. SS-Panzer-Division "Hitlerjugend"**, France, May 1944.

This tank showed a camouflage formed mainly by the *Olivgruen* colour, coupled to the standard *Dunkelgeld* and *Schokobraun*. Apparently, no markings were painted, except for the *Division* badge, on the right front fender. Only one antenna appears in the photo, a *Sternantenne D* mounted on the standard position for the 2 m pole antenna, at the rear left side of the superstructure.

Befehlspanzer • 55

Pz.Bef.Wg. IV Ausf.H, code "IN1", Nachr. Abt.130, **Panzer-Lehr-Division**, Normandy, June 1944.

Also this tank was fitted with a star antenna on the rear end of the left side, while the mount for the 2 m pole antenna was on the turret roof. The colour scheme included the three standard colours, with green and brown being oversprayed in wide bands and stripes. Markings were formed by the code "IN1", in black on the rear sides of the turret Schuerzen, while the national crosses, in black and white, were on the front part of the same Schuerzen. This tank was coated with Zimmerit, and was used by the Commander of II/Pz.Rgt.130, Major Prinz Wilhelm von Schoenburg-Waldenburg, KIA at Tilly-sur-Seulles on 11 June 1944.

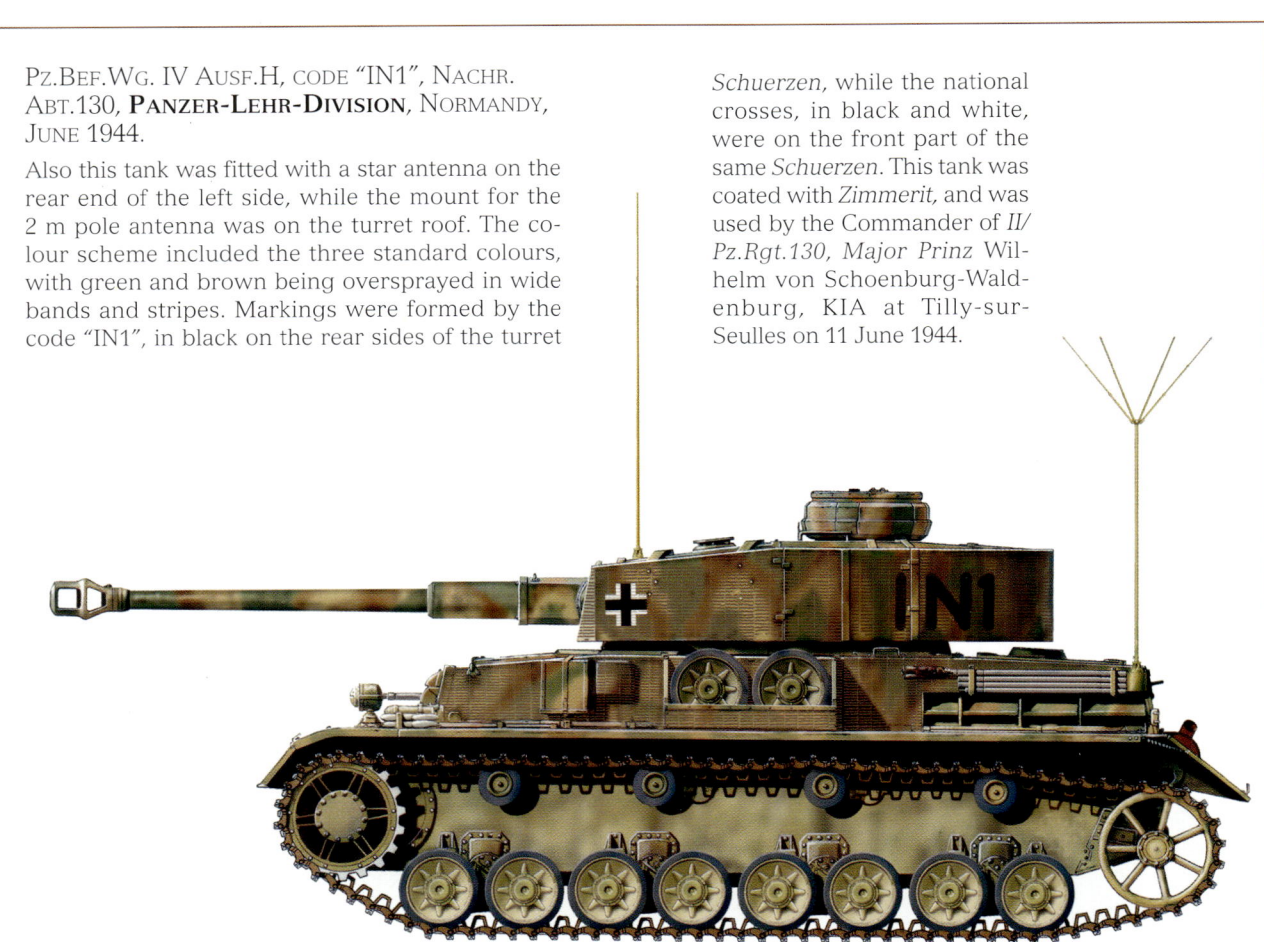

Pz.Bef.Wg. IV Ausf.H, code "779", Stab II/SS-Pz.Rgt.2, **2. SS-Panzer-Division "Das Reich"**, Normandy, July 1944.

This command tank was equipped with a 2 m pole antenna on the turret roof, and with a Sternantenne D on the rear end of the left side of the superstructure, in place of the standard 2 m antenna. The camouflage consisted in the classic three-colours scheme of dark yellow, olive-green and red-brown. Markings were formed by the code "779", in white outline, on the three positions of the turret Schuerzen, and by the German crosses, in black and white, on the sides of the front turret Schuerzen, and probably on the rear plate. This tank was coated with Zimmerit.

Pz.Bef.Wg. IV Ausf.H, code "II02", Stab II/Pz.Rgt.16, **116. Panzer-Division**, Normandy, August 1944.

This tank was fitted with a *Sternantenne D* on the right rear end of the rear plate, on the mount protected by an armoured pot, and maintained the standard 2 m pole antenna on the rear end, left side. The colour scheme was formed by bands of *Olivgruen* and *Schokobraun* over the *Dunkelgelb* base. Markings included the code "II02", in white, on the two rear sides of the turret *Schuerzen*, plus three national crosses, in black and white, on the sides and rear of the turret *Schuerzen*. This tank was coated with *Zimmerit*.

Pz.Bef.Wg. IV Ausf.H, code "II03", Stab II/SS-Pz.Rgt.3, **3. SS Panzer-Division "Totenkopf"**, Poland, August 1944.

The colour scheme of this tank was formed by the standard three colours, with bands of green and brown over the basic dark yellow. Markings included the code "II03" in white outline, on the sides and rear of the turret *Schuerzen*, plus the German crosses, in black and white, on the front of the turret *Schuerzen*. The antenna set is formed by a 2 m pole antenna at the standard position, plus a *Sternantenne D* at the right end of the rear plate. This tank was coated with *Zimmerit*.

Befehlspanzer • 57

BEFEHLSPZ.KPFW. IV AUSF.H, CODE "508", STAB PZ.ABT.2111, **PANZER-BRIGADE 111**, FRANCE, SEPTEMBER 1944.

This tank was transformed into a command tank thanks to the introduction of a Fu 8 radio set, associated to a *Sternantenne D* which was fitted to the right fender. The finish was in the three standard colours, with the basic *Dunkelgelb* oversprayed with stripes of *Olivgruen* and *Schokobraun*. Markings were formed by the code "508", handpainted in black, in four positions on the front and rear sides of the turret *Schurzen*, while on the front parts there were also the *Balkenkreutz*, in black and white. This tank was coated with *Zimmerit*.

PZ.BEF.WG. IV AUSF.J, UNKNOWN UNIT, FRANCE, SEPTEMBER 1944.

This tank (Fgst.Nr.92200) was one of only 17 Pz.Bef.Wg. IV Ausf .J of new production, completed in August-September 1944. It still had *Zimmerit,* and was equipped with two antennas, a 2m pole antenna on the turret roof, and a *Sternantenne D* on the right end of the rear plate. It was also equipped with a TSR.1 periscope (here in raised position) near the commander's cupola. No markings were present on this tank, while the colour scheme adopted was the *Hinterhalt-Tarnung*, (commonly known as "ambush camouflage"), applied at the factory, and formed in this case by wide bands and dots of *Olivgruen* and *Rotbraun* over the basic *Dunkelgelb*.

PANZER-BEOBACHTUNGSWAGEN IV AUSF.J, CODE "B1",
STAB-BTTR.(GEP) I/SS-PZ.ART-RGT.12 "HJ",
12.SS-PANZER-DIVISION "HITLERJUGEND",
BELGIUM, DECEMBER 1944.

The *Pz.Kpfw. IV* designed to artillery observation had three radio sets, and was equipped with three antennas: a *Sternantenne D* at the right end of the rear plate, plus two 2m antennas at the rear end of the left side, and on the turret roof. Markings for this tank included the code "B1", in black outlined white, on the rear sides of the turret *Schuerzen*, plus three *Balkenkreutz*, in black and white, on the front sides and rear of turret *Schuerzen*. The colour scheme was formed by a base of red oxide primer, overpainted with bands in *Dunkelgelb* and *Olivgruen*.

PZ.BEOB.WG. IV AUSF.J, CODE "201", STAB-BTTR.(GEP) I/PZ.ART.RGT. 4, **14.PANZER-DIVISION**, COURLAND, FEBRUARY 1945.

As for the previous profile, this artillery observation tank had three antennas, in the standard positions for the *Pz.Beob.Wg. IV*. However, the antenna on the turret roof is strange, as it was placed in the same position of the *Pz.Bef.Wg.IV Ausf.J*. Note the periscope of the TRS.1 sight, in raised position. The camouflage formed by the three standard colours was whitewashed, while the only visible marking was formed by the code "201", probably in *Olivgruen* outlined white, in the three classic positions on the turret *Schuerzen*. This tank was coated with *Zimmerit*

Befehlspanzer • 59

Pz.Kpfw.V chassis

PANZER-BEFEHLSWAGEN V PANTHER

The *Panther* is considered by many as the best tank design appeared during WWII, combining the best mix of firepower, mobility, and armour protection. It was born to reply to the threat posed by the Russian T-34 tank, and in the intentions of the German army, it was to become the standard combat vehicle of the *Panzer* units. Like the T-34 and the M4 Sherman, it can be considered as the "father" of the Main Battle Tank (MBT) concept.

However, since the very beginning, the *Panther* was designed to be declined also in a command and control version. In accordance with the need to conceal the identity of the command tanks, and with the need to simplify their production, the *Befehlspanther* was externally quite similar to the standard combat version. The only big difference from outside was the presence of two-three radio antennas, while other minor clues were the lack of the coaxial machine gun in the turret, and the stowage of additional extension rods for the *Sternantenne D* antenna just below the canister containing the gun cleaning rods, on the left side of the hull. Since July 1944, all the *Panther* tanks were produced with

▲ *Well known photo showing Befehlspanther Ausf.A coded "0", from the Stab of Pz.Rgt. "Grossdeutschland", taken in south Ukraine in January 1944. Note the 2 meters pole antenna on the turret roof, near the commander's cupola, and the Sternantenne D on the rear engine deck. In front of the tank, on the left, was Oberst Karl Lorenz, at the time Commander of Pz.Gren.Rgt. "GD", while Oberst Willy Langkeit, Commander of Pz.Rgt. "GD", is watching the scene from the tank's cupola. See profile at page 65.* (BA-101I-711-0427-04-Scheerer)

◄ *A Pz.Bef.Wg.V Panther Ausf.D/A from the Stab of II/SS-Pz.Rgt.5, from 5. SS-Panzer-Division "Wiking", taken on the eastern front, in March 1944. Note that the code "II02" was painted in white, but of a darker shade than the whitewash. This tank was equipped with two pole antennas, thus having quite probably an Sd.Kfz.268 radio configuration.* (Museum Wojska Pollskiego via WM)

▲ Panther tanks of I/Pz.Rgt.4 taken in Tuscany, Italy, in summer 1944. In the foreground is Pz.Bef.Wg.V Ausf.D/A coded "102". Note the star antenna on the engine deck, and the additional antenna sections stowed on the hull side, under the tube containing the gun cleaning set. The code was red outlined white, while the tank was painted in Dunkelgelb overall, and covered with Zimmerit. (BA-101I-478-2164-39-Bayer))

the necessary brackets and plugs to convert them (if required) into command tanks on the field, and the *Panzer* maintenance units were provided with specific kits for this purpose.

The standard *Panther* tank was equipped with one radio set, an Fu 5, while the tanks assigned to Company or Platoon commanders had one Fu 5 and one Fu 2 radio sets, but only with one antenna. The *Befehls* models were declined in two different variants, the *Sd.kfz.267* and *268*. The first was destined to *Abteilung* and *Regiment* headquarters, and was fitted with one Fu 8 set, located in the right front hull, in the same position of the Fu 5 of the standard tanks, and one Fu 5, which was moved inside the right side of the turret, near the loader position. The Fu 8 was associated to a 1.8 meters *Sternantenne D* antenna, which was fitted to a porcelain insulator, protected by an armoured cylinder (*Panzertopf*), located in the middle of the rear engine deck. The Fu 5 was connected to a 2 meters *Stabantenne* (pole antenna) whose base was located on the rear right side of the turret roof. The *Sd.Kfz.268* was destined to provide aero-cooperation, maintaining contact with the Luftwaffe air units, and was assigned to the so-called *Flivo* (*Flieger-Verbindugsoffizier*, or ground-to-air liaison officer). In this version, the Fu 8 was replaced by an Fu 7, which was associated to a 1.4 meters antenna, fitted to the left side of the engine deck, using the same base of the Fu 5 antenna for the standard tanks. This second version was produced in low numbers, and seldom used, as in the final years of the war the *Luftwaffe* air units were rarely present and capable to support the land forces. To provide better communications on long ranges, the *Sternantenne D* could be prolonged thanks to three 1.25 meters extension rods stowed on the left side of the hull. In this configuration, usable only in static positions, the *Sternantenne* could be secured to the rear plate of the hull, using some connections located near the right stowage canister. However,

▼ A Befehlspanther Ausf.D/A from the Stab of SS-Pz.Rgt.12 taken during an exercise in Belgium, in spring 1944. Note that the antennas are not fitted in the standard bases, as the Sternantenne D is on the left side of the engine deck. This tank showed no codes or markings. In the commader's cupola was SS-Obersturmbannfuehrer Max Wuensche, at the time Commander of SS-Pz.Rgt.12 "HJ". (US NARA)

in the field, these combinations of antennas were not always the standard, and it wasn't uncommon to see *Sternantenne D* mounted on the left side of the engine deck, instead that on the *Panzertopf* position, on the rear. This was common especially to the *Befehlspanther* converted from standard tanks at the front, by the maintenance units, as replacement for the assigned command tanks lost for various reasons during combat operations. Some command *Panther* were seen also mounting three antennas, even if usually only two were necessary.

Other differences from the standard *Panther* tanks were the presence in the combat room of a GG400 auxiliary generator, to provide the radios with the necessary power; the removal of the coaxial machine gun in the turret (and the closure of the opening in the gun shield with a welded plug); the reduction of the main 7.5 cm ammunitions (15 rounds less in the *Ausf.D* and A models, 12 rounds in the *Ausf.G*), and the removal of machine gun accessories, in order to make room for the equipment associated to the new radios. In the *Panther Ausf. A* there was also the removal of the loader's auxiliary turret traverse mechanism.

The crew of the *Befehlspanther* was composed by a commander, a communication officer/gunner, a radio operator/loader, a radio operator/machine gunner, and a driver.

A total of 329 *Befehlspanther* were produced in the period May 1943-April 1945, all manufactured by MAN. This version was not part of dedicated contracts, but was mixed in the normal production run, so no specific lists or *Fahrgestell* numers exist. In total, MAN produced 242 Panther *Ausf.D* (Fgst.Nr. 210001-210254), 645 *Ausf.A* (210255-

◀ A Pz.Bef.Wg.V Panther Ausf.A *code "R02" from the* Stab *of* SS-Pz.Rgt.1, 1. SS-Panzer-Division "LSSAH", *taken in France before the battle of Normandy. Note that the photographer carefully avoided to include in the shot the star antenna, on the rear. Note also the lack of the coaxial MG on the gun mantlet. See profile at page 67.* (BA via JR)

210899) and about 1,143 *Ausf.G* (120301-121443), for a total of 2,030 tanks out of the about 6,003 produced by all the five industries (MAN, Daimler-Benz, Henschel, MNH, Demag) involved in the *Panther* program. The first unit to be-requipped with the new tank was *Panzer-Abteilung 51*, which was established on 9 January 1943, following the re-naming of *II.Abteilung/Panzer-Regiment 33*, coming from *9. Panzer-Division*. It was followed on 6 February 1943 by *Panzer-Abteilung 52*, converted from *I.Abteilung/Panzer-Regiment 15*, from *11.Panzer-Division*. Each of these battalions received a full outfit of 96 *Panther*. They were joined under *Panzer-Regiment 39*, which deployed 200 Panthers, nine of them being *Befehlspanther*, three each assigned to the *Regiment* and to the two *Abteilung* Headquarters. This unit was prepared with the aim to launch it in operation "Zitadelle", the battle for the Kursk bulge, and was deployed to the Eastern front by early July 1943. After the battle of Kursk, many other *Panther* units were re-equipped and sent to combat on all fronts, and fought until the end of the war. According to the *K.St.N. 1103* of 1 November 1943 and *K.St.N. 1150a* of 10 January 1943, the *Nachrichten-Zug* of each *Panzer-Regiment* had to receive three *Befehlspanther*, and the *Nachrichten-Zug* of each *Panther* Battalion had to receive two *Befehlspanther* (plus one standard *Panther*). *K.St.N. 1150a* of 1 November 1943 raised to three the *Befehlspanther* for the *Nachr.Zug*. of the *Panther* Battalion, and this was confirmed also in the *K.St.N. 1107 (freie Gliederung)* of 1 November 1944. However, on 1 April 1945, *K.St.N 1103a* assigned only two *Befehlspanther* to the Stab of the *gemischten Panzer-Regiment*, and *K.St.N. 1107* of 1 April 1945 assigned two *Befehlspanther* to the *Nachr.Zug*. of the *Panzer-Abteilung "Panther" (freie Gliederung)*, probably confirming on paper what was already become a forced common practise on the ground.

PANZER-BEOBACHTUNGSWAGEN V PANTHER

To provide a feasible armoured vehicle to the artillery forward observation officers of the self-propelled artillery units, the German Army introduced into service in Spring 1943 modified versions of its outdated *Pz.Kpfw.III*, mostly rebuilt tanks from *Ausf.F* and *G* models. This had to be a stop-gap measure, waiting for the development of a dedicated vehicle, that had to be realized starting from the basis of the new *Pz.Kpfw.V Panther Ausf.D*. Studies started as early as November 1942, and first drawings appeared in March 1943. Different proposals were made, concerning a new turret design, to be installed in a standard *Panther* chassis. The drawings of this turret were completed and reviewed by 16 July 1943. The project was based on a dedicated turret, developed from that of the *Panther Ausf.D*, with some features coming from the *Ausf. A*. The general shape was that of the *Ausf.D* turret, but the front was completely different. It was formed by a flat 100 mm thick plate, which on the left supported a bolted fake gun and gun shield, while on the right housed the only arma-

Pz.Bef.Wg. V (Sd.Kfz.267 and 268) Ausf. A: specifications

LENGTH:	8.86 M
WIDTH:	3.44
HEIGHT:	2.99 M
WEIGHT (COMBAT):	45.5 T
ENGINE:	V12 WATER-COOLED 23.1 LT GASOLINE, DELIVERING 700 HP AT 3,000 RPM
FUEL CAPACITY:	730 LT
TRANSMISSION:	ZF AK7-200, WITH 1 REVERSE AND 7 FORWARD GEAR
MAX SPEED:	55 KM/H
RANGE (ON ROAD):	200 KM
RANGE (CROSS COUNTRY):	100 KM
GRADE:	?°
TRENCH CROSSING:	1.9 M
STEP:	90 CM
FORDING DEPTH:	190 CM
GROUND CLEARANCE:	56 CM
GROUND PRESSURE:	0.73 KG/CM2
POWER RATIO:	15.5 HP/TON
WEAPONS:	1 x 7.5 CM KW.K. 42 (L/70) 2 x 7.92MM MG.34 MACHINE GUN
AMMUNITION:	64 (GUN)
PROTECTION:	HULL FRONT: 80-60 MM TURRET FRONT: 100 MM
COMMUNICATIONS:	1 x Fu 5, 1 x Fu 8 (SdKfz.267), 1 x Fu 5, 1 x Fu 7 (SdKfz.268)
CREW:	5

▶ *A Befehlspanther Ausf.D code "155", from the* Stab *of I/SS-Pz.Rgt.9 "H", taken in Normandy in July 1944. Note the presence of three antennas, but the* Sternantenne D *was on the left side of the engine deck. The additional antenna sections are stowed on the hull side, under the tube containing the gun cleaning set. See profile at page 68. (BA via JR)*

▼ *A Pz.Bef.Wg.V Panther Ausf.A taken in Normandy, near Soumont-Saint-Quentin, in August 1944. It belonged probably to SS-Pz.Rgt.12. Note the star antenna fitted on the left side of the engine deck, while no markings are visible (except for the* Balkenkreuz*), also because of the ample stowage on the turret side. (Schultz via JR)*

▼▼ *A Befehlspanther Ausf.G destroyed by British Shermans from 44th RTR near the town of Erp, Holland, during Operation "Market-Garden", on 23 September 1944. This tank was the mount of Major Hans-Albrecht von Pluskow, Commander of Pz.Abt. 2107, from Panzer-Brigade 107. It had a standard radio configuration, but with three antennas. (US NARA)*

ment of the tank, a ball mount for an MG.34 machine gun. On the far left and right ends of the front plate there were two openings for the sights of a stereoscopic rangefinder. On the turret roof there was one hatch for the observation periscope plus, at the rear end, the mount for a radio antenna. On the engine deck there was the *Sternantenne D* for the Fu 8 of Fu 4 radio sets, with the same position and fittings as in the *Befehlspanther*. The radio set was completed by a *Funksprechgeraet f* system, dedicated to communicate with the artillery batteries.

Specific mission equipment of this vehicle were a Zeiss EM 1.25m stereoscopic range finder, a TBF 2 observation periscope (mounted in the turret roof, in a ball mounting, it could be raised and lowered), a TSR 1 spotting periscope, a SF14Z scissors periscope, and a KZF 2 telescopic gun sight. The TRS 1 and the SF14Z could be mounted alternatively on an adjustable bracket inside the commander's cupola. The latter was a feature coming from the *Ausf. A* model, and was equipped with seven periscopes. Other helps to the artillery officers were azimuth indicators for the commander and the observer, and an *Anschuetz Blockstelle 0* plotting board, destined to give initial range and line, and fire corrections, in areas were maps were not available or incorrect. It was located inside the turret, in front of the commander's cupola position.

According to the most accurate information, only one prototype of *Panzer-Beobachtungswagen Panther* was assembled, using a prototype turret coupled to a *Ausf.D* chassis, produced in the period July-September 1943. This vehicle was used for test and evaluation activity, but the type was never approved for series production. According to a note of 31 March 1944 in the war diary of *General der Artillerie* Lindemann, the question to equip artillery units with *Panther* tanks was strongly opposed by the *Panzerwaffe*. As a matter of fact, the *General-Inspekteur der Panzertruppen* wanted to use all the available production to equip *Panzer* units, and no *Panther* chassis was ever authorized to be diverted to satisfy the needs of the Artillery. ❑

Pz.Bef.Wg.V Ausf.D, code "R01", Stab Pz.Rgt. 39, **Panzer-Brigade 10**, Ukraine, July 1943.

This early *Ausf.D* had a colour scheme formed by the standard factory finish in *Dunkelgelb*, oversprayed at the unit by stripes of *Olivgruen*. Markings include the code "R01", in black outlined white, on the turret sides and rear, plus a German national cross, in black and white, in the middle of the rear plate.

Pz.Bef.Wg.V Ausf.D, code "I01", Stab **Panzer-Abteilung 51** attached to **Panzer-Grenadier-Division "Grossdeutschland"**, Ukraine, August 1943.

This tank was part of the second assignment of *Panther* to *Pz.Abt.51* after the battle of Kursk, and it was left in *Dunkelgelb* overall. Markings were different from those used at Kursk, and included the code "I01" in black on the upper front sides of the turret, and on the rear, coupled to the silhouette of a panther, stencilled in black, on the lower front part of the turret sides. The German cross was black and white in the middle of the rear plate.

Pz.Bef.Wg.V Ausf.D, code "I01", Stab I/Panzer-Regiment 15, **11. Panzer-Division**, Ukraine, late 1943.

This tank received a wide overspray mottle in *Olivgruen* and *Schokobraun* over the factory *Dunkelgelb*. Markings include the code "I01", in black outlined white, on the turret sides and rear, plus the German *Balkenkreuz*, in black and white, in the middle of the rear plate. Note the presence of three radio antennas, even if the *Pz.Bef.Wg.V* was equipped with only two radio sets.

Pz.Bef.Wg.V Ausf.A, code "0", Stab Pz.Rgt. "GD", **Panzer-Grenadier-Division "Grossdeutschland"**, Ukraine, January 1944.

This Panther received an accurate whitewash over the normal finish in *Dunkelgelb* and *Olivgruen*. The visible markings were the code "0", in black, on the turret side and rear, flaked by a small *Stahlhelm* (steel helmet) in black, the *Division* badge. The national cross, in black outlined white, was painted on the two front corners of the hull sides.

Befehlspanzer • 65

Pz.Bef.Wg.V Ausf.A, code "II01", Stab II/Pz-Rgt.23, **23.Panzer-Division**, Russia, January 1944.

This tank had a winter whitewash over the normal three-tone camouflage. The only visible marking was the code "II01", handpainted in black on the turret sides, and probably rear. The national cross, in black and white, was painted on the front hull sides.

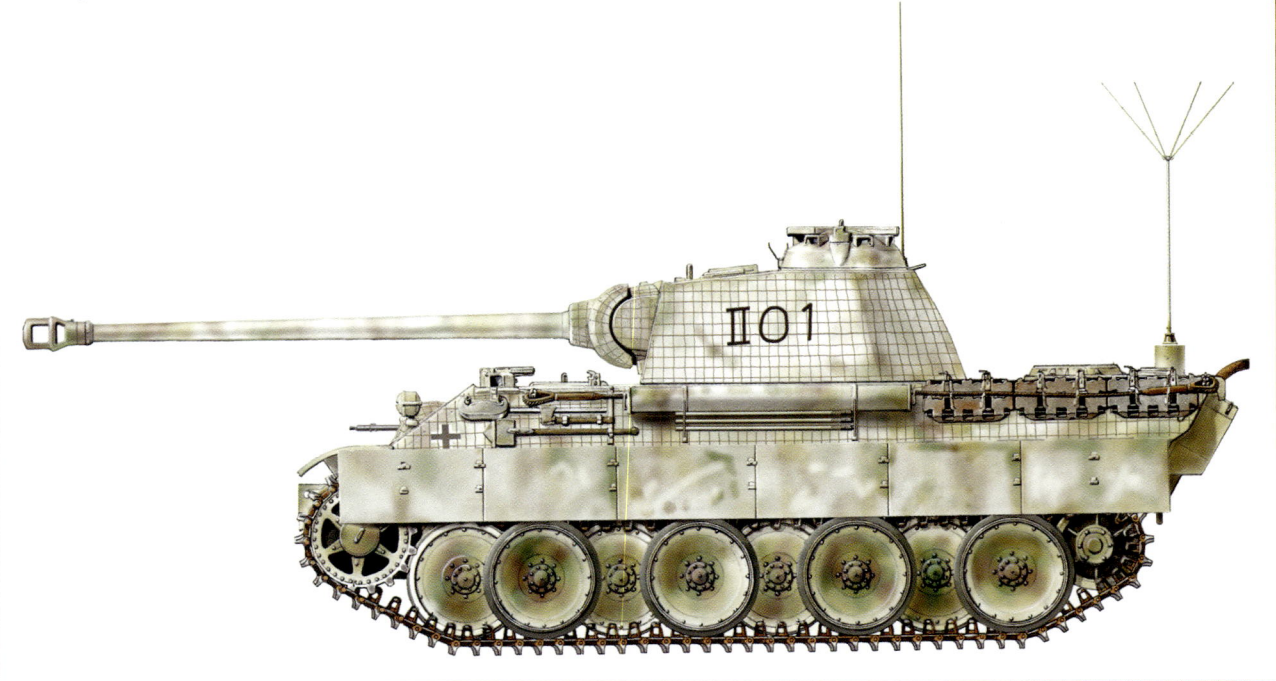

Pz.Bef.Wg.V Ausf.D, code "I02", Stab **I/Pz-Rgt.4**, Italy, February 1944.

This command tank was finished overspraying wide bands of *Olivgruen* on the factory *Dunkelgelb*. Markings included the code "I02", in white outline, on the turret sides and rear, plus the German national crosses, in black and white, on the front corners of the hull side, and in the middle of the rear plate. This tank was equipped with a *Sternantenne D* on the rear engine deck, plus two 2 m pole antennas, on the turret roof, and on the standard position, on the left front side of the engine deck.

66 • *Befehlspanzer*

Pz.Bef.Wg.V Ausf.A, code "I03", probably Stab I/Pz-Rgt.2, **16.Panzer-Division**, Russia, spring 1944.

The camouflage of this tank appeared to be formed by wide bands of *Olivgruen* oversprayed on the basic *Dunkelgelb* finish. Hull and turret were coated with *Zimmerit*, while the markings included only the code "I03", in red, on the turret sides and rear.

Pz.Bef.Wg.V Ausf.A, code "R02", Stab SS-Pz-Rgt.1 "LSSAH", **1.SS-Panzer-Division "LSSAH"**, Normandy, June 1944.

This tank received a wide series of patches in olive-green and red-brown on the standard *Dunkelgelb* finish. Markings were quite unusual: The code "R02", in white outline, was painted on the side *Schuerzen* and on the rear of the turret, while on the turret sides, in an area scratched from *Zimmerit*, it was painted a black panther jumping in a yellow circle, with a lightning in the middle. In the rear sides of the turret, the *Zimmerit* was engraved with the letters "LSSAH". The German national crosses were in black and white, on the front corners of the hull, and probably on the right stowage box of the rear plate.

Pz.Bef.Wg.V Ausf.A, code "I02", Stab **I/Pz-Rgt.24**, attached to the **116. Panzer-Division**, Normandy, late July 1944.

This tank had the typical camouflage scheme of this Abteilung in summer 1944: bands of Olivgruen, Rotbraun and Dunkelgelb painted on the basic Dunkelgelb. Markings were formed by the code "I02", in white, on the turret sides and rear, plus the German crosses, in black and white, on the front corners of the hull. The spare wheel on the turret rear sides and the move of the tube of gun cleaning set from the hull side to the rear engine deck, were typical of this unit.

Pz.Bef.Wg.V Ausf.D, code "155", Stab I/SS-Pz-Rgt.9 "H", **9. SS-Panzer-Division "Hohenstaufen"**, Normandy, July 1944.

This late *Ausf.D* model did not receive any camouflage scheme besides the standard factory *Dunkelgelb* overall. Markings included the code "155", in white, on the turret sides and rear, plus the usual German crosses, in black and white, on the front corners of the hull. This tank was equipped with three antennas.

Pz.Bef.Wg.V Ausf.A, code "96", Stab/II Pz-Rgt.33, **9. Panzer-Division**, Normandy, August 1944.

As many vehicles on the Western front, also this tank was camouflaged with a three-tone scheme of red-brown and olive-green on the basic sand-yellow. The only visible markings were the code "96", in white, on the rear of the turret, and the Balkenkreuz, in black and white, on the front corners of the hull.

Pz.Bef.Wg.V Ausf.A, code "R02", Stab SS-Pz-Rgt.5 "W", **5. SS-Panzer-Division "Wiking"**, Poland, August 1944.

This tank, used by the commander of *SS-Pz-Rgt.5, Standartenfuehrer* Muehlenkamp, was camouflaged with brushed *Olivgruen* and *Schokobraun* stripes on the standard *Dunkelgelb*. Markings were the code "R02", in white, on the turret sides and rear, plus the usual German *Balkenkreuz* on the front corners of the hull.

Pz.Bef.Wg.V Ausf.A, code "N1", Stab I/Pz-Rgt. "GD", **Panzer-Grenadier-Division "Grossdeutschland"**, Latvia, August 1944.

The camouflage of this vehicle was typical of the period for this unit, and consisted of wide bands of olive-green and red-brown in splinter scheme on the usual dark-yellow base. The code "N1" was white outlined black, on the turret sides and rear, while a pale *Balkenkreuz* in black and white was painted on the front corners of the hull. This tank was coated with *Zimmerit*.

Pz.Bef.Wg. Panther mit Pz.Kpfw.IV turm, Stab **schwere Panzerjaeger-Abteilung 653**, Ukraine, summer 1944.

This tank was the result of a heavy field modification, destined to provide a new command tank to the unit. The maintenance shop of *s.Pz.Jg.Abt. 653* used the hull of a *Bergepanther* recovery tank, and casted on it in fixed position the turret coming from a destroyed *Pz.Kpfw.IV Ausf.H*. The camouflage scheme was a classic three-tone, while the markings included only the German cross, in black and white, painted on the turret *Schuerzen*. The antenna set included a *Sternatenne D* on the engine deck, and a 2 m pole antenna in the standard position for *Panther* tanks.

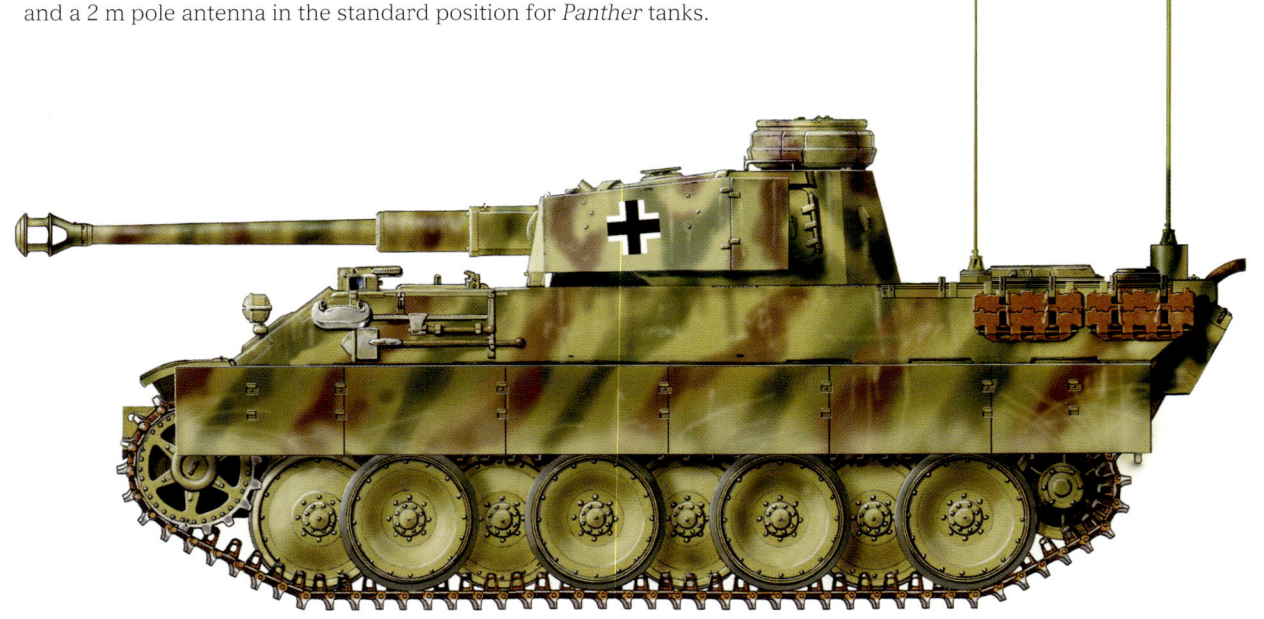

Pz.Bef.Wg.V Ausf.D, code "II01", Stab II/SS-Pz-Rgt.5 "W",
5. SS-Panzer-Division "Wiking", Poland, summer 1944.

The camouflage colours of this tank were formed by a light mottle of olive-green and red-brown oversprayed on the basic sand-yellow. The identification markings included the code "II01", in white, on the turret sides and rear, while the German crosses, in black and white, were painted on the front corners of the hull. To be noted that on the front part of the turret sides a *Zimmerit* area was lay in form of a shield, possibly to receive the *Division* badge, which however was not painted.

Pz.Bef.Wg.V Ausf.G, code "I03", Stab I/SS-Pz-Rgt.3 "T",
3. SS-Panzer-Division "Totenkopf", Poland, August 1944.

The colour scheme of this tank was formed by a mottle of *Olivgruen* and *Schokobraun* over the basic *Dunkelgelb,* all over the *Zimmerit* coating. Markings included the code "I03", in white, on the turret sides and rear, while near it, on the turret sides, there were also the *Balkenkreuz*, in black and white.

Befehlspanzer • 71

Pz.Bef.Wg.V Ausf.G, code "I82", Stab I/Pz-Rgt.35, **4. Panzer-Division**, Poland, summer 1944.

The colour scheme of this vehicle was formed by wide areas of olive-green and red-brown, over the basic sand-yellow. Also this tank was coated with *Zimmerit*. Markings were formed by the code "I82", in yellow, on the turret sides and rear, plus the German crosses, in black and white, on the turret sides. Note that this tank was equipped with three antennas.

Pz.Bef.Wg.V Ausf.G, code "IN3", Stab **I/Pz-Rgt.26**, attached to **Panzer-Grenadier-Division "Grossdeutschland"**, Latvia, summer 1944.

This tank, which was coated with *Zimmerit*, was camouflaged with the only basic *Dunkelgelb* colour, applied at the factory. Markings included the code "IN3", in black outlined white, on the turret sides and rear, plus the German crosses, in black and white, on the turret sides, and rear hull plate. On the front part of the turret it was painted also the battalion badge, a black panther's head.

Pz.Bef.Wg.V Ausf.G, code "003", Stab **schwere Panzerjaeger-Abteilung 654,** France, November 1944.

This tank was one of those which, under the new rules of August 1944, were camouflaged directly at the factory, with wide bands of *Olivgruen* and *Rotbraun* over the basic *Dunkelgelb*. Markings included the code "003", in red outlined white, on the turret sides, and rear, plus the *Balkenkreuz*, in black and white, on the front hull sides, in the middle of the front and of the rear hull plates, and on the rear left stowage box.

Pz.Bef.Wg.V Ausf.G, code "002", Stab SS-Pz-Rgt.1 "LSSAH", **1. SS-Panzer-Division "LSSAH",** Belgium, December 1944.

This tank was camouflaged at the factory, with a scheme of wide bands of olive-green, red-brown, and sand-yellow, over the basic red oxide primer. The markings were formed by the code "002", in black, painted small on the sides of the gun shield, and on the turret rear, plus the *Balkenkreuz*, in black and white, on the turret sides. This tank had no *Zimmerit*, and was equipped with three antennas.

Pz.Bef.Wg.V Ausf.G, code "151", Stab I/SS-Pz-Rgt.1 "LSSAH",
1. SS-Panzer-Division "LSSAH", Belgium, December 1944.

Like in the previous profile, also this tank was produced in autumn 1944, and received the camouflage scheme, in the standard three colours, directly at the MAN factory. The markings were formed by the code "151", in black outlined white with a stencil, painted on the turret sides and rear, plus the *Balkenkreuz*, in black and white, on the turret sides.

Pz.Bef.Wg.V Ausf.G, code "99", Stab SS-Pz-Rgt.2 "DR",
2. SS-Panzer-Division "Das Reich", Belgium, January 1945.

Also this tank was one of those produced by MAN in autumn 1944, and destined to re-equip the *Panzer* units before the start of Operation *"Wacht Am Rhein"*, the Battle of the Bulge; the colour scheme is the same of the other two previous profiles. The code "99" was black outlined white, on the turret sides and rear, while no German national crosses were present of the sides or on the turret.

Pz.Bef.Wg.V Ausf.G, code "R01", Stab Pz-Rgt. "HG", **Fallschirjaeger-Panzer-Division "Hermman Goering"**, Prussland, January 1945.

This tank had the standard camouflage scheme of the three colours applied at the factory, but interestingly is equipped with *Schuerzen* which sport the *Hinterhalt* colour scheme, of MAN origin, which was used to be painted at the factory in September 1944. The code "R01" was red outlined white, on the turret sides, while the *Balkenkreuz* were painted on the front sides of the hull. On the front plate there was the construction number (121081) in black, and a personal badge, a centaur, in white.

Pz.Bef.Wg.V Ausf.G, code "AJ9", Stab SS-Pz-Rgt.9 "H", **9. SS-Panzer-Division "Hohenstaufen"**, Hungary, March 1945.

Also this tank had a standard colour scheme applied by MAN, but in this case with the base colour being the *Olivegruen*, as ordered on 20 December 1944. The code "AJ9" (meaning *Adjutant* SS-Pz-Rgt.9) was painted in black outlined white, on the turret sides, while the *Balkenkreuz* were on the front sides of the hull. This tank was equipped with three antennas.

Pz.Bef.Wg.V Ausf.G, code "965", Stab Pz-Rgt.1, **1. Panzer-Division**, Hungary, March 1945.

This *Panther* was featured by a faded whitewash (probably removed by the crew with the melting of the snow) over the standard three-colors camouflage. The code "965" was in red outlined white, with a bar of the same style (of unknown meaning) under the digit 9. Near the code there was the *Balkenkreuz*, in black and red, a practice appeared in the last weeks of the War, probably to make the marking less visible. This tank was equipped only with a single *Sternantenned D*, on the normal base on the left front side of the engine deck, meaning that this was quite probably a standard tank converted on the field to command tasks.

Pz.Beob.Wg.V Panther, Germany, autumn 1943.

This profile shows the prototype of the *Panther* designed to be used as artillery observation tank. The hull was that of a *Panther Ausf.D*, while the turret was specifically designed for the task, and was featured by a fake gun tube, and by a commander's cupola adopted on the *Ausf.A* model. Besides this sample, no other *Beobachtungspanther* were ever transformed, or built.

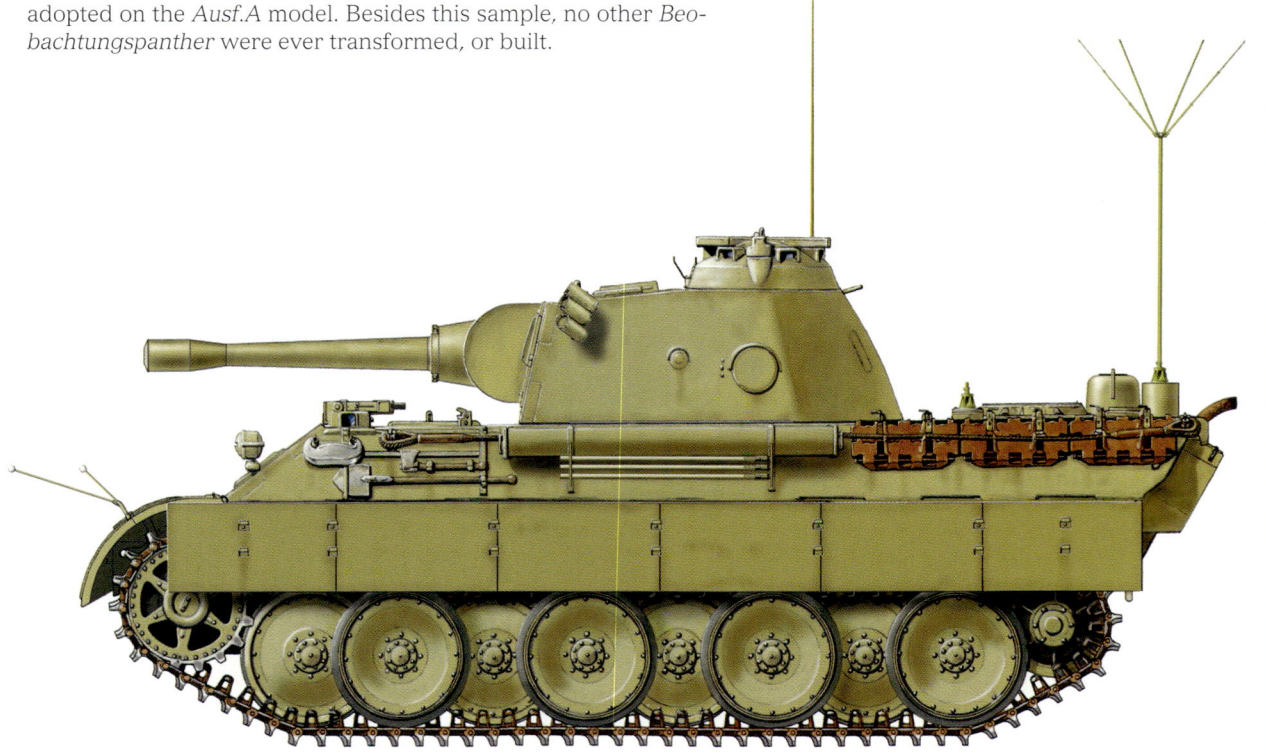

Pz.Kpfw.VI chassis

Panzer-Befehlswagen VI Tiger

As happened for other German tanks produced after 1941, also the new heavy tank *Tiger* was designed since the beginning to be produced also in a command version, with only minor differences from the standard combat tank, in order to simplify production, ease the assembly activity, hide to the enemy the identity of the command tanks from distance, and provide the field maintenance units the capability to easily convert standard tanks into command tanks when required.

Production of the *Tiger Ausf.H* and *E* (Sd.Kfz.181, or Tiger I) by Henschel started in August 1942, and continued until August 1944, with a total of 1,346 tanks completed (Fgst.Nr. 250001-251346). In total, 89 of these were *Befehlstigers*, which were produced in *Sd.Kfz.267* and *Sd.Kfz.268* versions, from February 1943 (three completed) until August 1944. On 11 October 1943, an order was issued to complete one *Befehlstiger* every 20 standard tank, but this never happened.

As for the *Panther* tank, modifications introduced with the command model were few. The tank did not receive the coaxial MG.34 machine gun in the turret, including its accessories (spare barrel, tool box, sight, bipod, 1,500 rounds of ammunition, belt bags), one baggage box on the right front of the turret, and 26 rounds of ammunition for the 8.8 cm KwK 36 L/56 gun, with their stowage brackets.

The standard *Tiger I* tanks were fitted with one *Bordsprechanlage* set (intercom system), and one Fu 5 radio set, while the tanks assigned to Platoon and Company command had one Fu 5 and one Fu 2 radio sets.

The radio sets for the *Befehlstiger* were fitted in two positions: the Fu 5 set was mounted in the right side of the turret, near the loader's position, while the associated 2 m *Stabantenne* was mounted in the turret roof. The loader seat was replaced by a *Pz-Funkersitz*, a seat for a radio operator. The Fu 7 or Fu 8 radio sets were located to the left of the radio operator in the front part of the hull. The antenna for the Fu 7 set (used in the *Sd.Kfz.268* version) was a 1.4 m *Stabantenne* mounted on the left side of the engine deck, near the turret, while the antenna for the Fu 8 (for the *Sd.Kfz.267* version), the usual *Sternantenne D* of 1.8 m, was mounted on the right side of the engine deck, near the turret. The radio sets were completed by the presence of a *Bordsprechanlage B fuer Panzerbefehlswagen*, the intercom set B for command tanks. Inside the combat room there was the GG400 auxiliary generator set, proving power to the radios, and the radio accessory box. The three 1.25 m extension rods for the *Sternantenne D* were stowed in a tube fitted to the left side of the rear hull plate, and they could be used for long range static communications.

▶ A Befehlstiger Ausf.H *from the* Stab *of* s.H.Pz.Abt.505 *taken in Ukraine, in June 1943, before the battle of Kursk. The code "II", indicating the second tank in the Battalion HQ, is clearly visible on the turret side.* (copyright reserved, via JR)

▲ *Mechanics at work around a Pz.Bef.Wg.VI Tiger Ausf.H coded "A2", from the* Stab *of* s.H.Pz.Abt.508*, taken in Italy, in March 1944. Note the presence of two antennas, on the turret roof and on the right side of the hull, plus the tube containing the additional antenna sections, fitted to the left side of the rear hull.* (BA-101I-311-0904-39A-Vack)

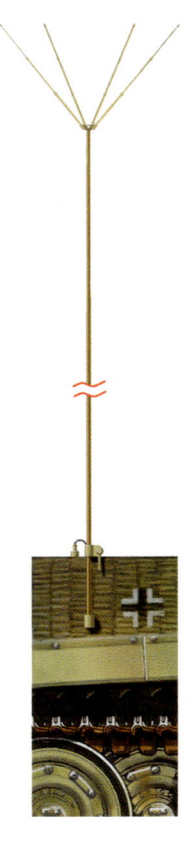

◀ Befehlstiger Ausf.E *code "009" from the* Stab *of* s.SS.Pz.Abt.101 *taken in Normandy, in July 1944. Note on the hull side the presence of the two connections destined to support the additional antenna sections for the* Sternantenne D, *when in static position for long range communications. In the drawing it is possible to see the configuration with the additional sections. (BA via JR)*

companies detached to various Divisions. In such cases it was not uncommon that Company commanders used *Befehlstiger* in order to maintain communications with the Battalion Headquarters, especially in the Russian and Italian theatres, were long distances and mountains made the radio communications more difficult.

The first two units destined to be equipped with the *Tiger I* were the *schwere-Panzer-Kompanie 501* and *502*, established on 16 February 1942. Later, they were both assigned to the *schwere-Panzer-Abteilung 501* (*s.Pz. Abt.501*), established on 10 May 1942. In the same period two more battalions were formed: *s.Pz.Abt.503* (5 May

In this case, the whole antenna was mounted on two connections located on the right side of the hull, near the standard position. In addition, other modifications included the vision slit in the right side of the turret and the opening for the coaxial machine-gun in the gun shield, both closed with welded armour plugs. Later in the war, also the loader's periscope opening in the turret roof was sealed.

The crew of the *Befehlstiger* was formed by a *Kommandeur* (commander), a *Nachrichtenoffizier-Richtschuetze* (signal officer/gunner), a *Panzerfunker 1-Ladeschuetze* (radio operator 1/loader), a *Panzerfunker 2* (radio operator 2), and a *Fahrer* (driver).

According to *K.St.N. 1150b* of 15 August 1942, the *Stab-Kompanie* of each *schwere-Panzer-Abteilung* had to receive two *Befehlstiger* (and six *Pz.Kpfw.III*). On 5 March 1943, the new *K.St.N. 1150e* for the *schwere-Panzer-Abteilung "Tiger"* included again only two *Befehlstiger* (plus one standard *Tiger*) in the *Nachrichten-Zug* of the *Stabs-Kompanie*. The *K.St.N. 1150e* of 1 November 1943 increased to three the number of *Befehlstiger* assigned to the signal Platoon of the command Company. The same organization was confirmed by the *K.St.N. 1107b freie Gliederung (fG)*, of 1 June 1944, and by the *K.St.N 1107d(fG)* of 1 November 1944. However, it must be recalled that the *Tiger* Battalions were usually assigned to *Panzerkorps* units, and their

Pz.Bef.Wg. Tiger (Sd.Kfz.267 and 268) Ausf. E: specifications	
Length:	8.45 m
Width:	3.70 m
Height:	3.00 m
Weight (combat):	57 t
Engine:	Maybach HK230P45 V12 Water-cooled 23.8 lt gasoline, delivering 700 HP at 3,000 rpm
Fuel capacity:	540 lt
Transmission:	Maybach-Olvar OG40 12 16A, with 4 reverse and 8 forward gear
Max speed:	45 km/h
Range (on road):	195 km
Range (cross country):	110 km
Grade:	?
Trench crossing:	2.50 m
Step:	79 cm
Fording Depth:	160 cm
Ground clearance:	47 cm
Ground pressure:	0.74 kg/cm2
Power ratio:	12.3 HP/ton
Weapons:	1 x 8.8 cm Kw.K. 36 (L/56) 2 x 7.92mm MG.34 machine gun
Ammunition:	66 (gun)
Protection:	hull front: 100 mm turret front: 120-100 mm
Communications:	1 x Fu 5, 1 x Fu 8 (SdKfz.267), 1 x Fu 5, 1 x Fu 7 (SdKfz.268))
Crew:	5

▶ *Tiger tanks of the* s.H.Pz.Abt.506 *taken on a train that brought them to Russia, in September 1943. The one on the foreground is a* Pz.Bef.Wg.VI Ausf.H, *as shown by the presence of a pole antenna on the turret roof. The "W" letter of the badge painted on* Rommelkiste *was in green, colour of the* Stab. (copyright reserved, via JR)

▶▼ *A view from the rear of* Befehlstiger Ausf.B *code "502", from* s.H.Pz.Abt.501, *which shows the armoured pot for the* Sternantenne D, *located in the middle of the rear engine deck, and immediately below it, horizontally, the tube containing the additional antenna sections. On the turret roof it is possible to see the mount for the 2 meters pole antenna, on the right edge. Curiously, a 2 meter pole antenna is fitted on the usual position for a standard tank, on the right side of the engine deck. This was an early Tiger II, still covered with Zimmerit.* (copyright reserved, via JR)

▶▼▼ *One of the three* Befehlstiger Ausf.B *assigned to* s.H.Pz.Abt.506 *was "03", here taken at Villers-la-Bonne-Eau, near Bastogne, in January 1945, having been captured by the US Army, after Operation "Wacht am Rhein", the Battle of the Bulge.* (US NARA)

1942), and *s.Pz.Abt.502* (25 May 1942). These were the first three units to receive also *Befehlstigers*, when deliveries of the new tank started, in June 1942. The first unit to see combat (*s.Pz.Abt.502*) was sent to the Russian front in August 1942. The second unit to be committed to combat operations was *s.Pz.Abt.501*, which arrived at Bizerte, Tunisia, from 23 November 1942.

It's probable that during the war, some *Befehlstigers* were realized through workshop conversions on the field. However, it's interesting to note that in November 1943, 18 *Befehlstiger* were converted back to standard *Tiger I* combat tanks.

Panzer-Befehlswagen Tiger Ausf.B

The *Panzerbefehlswagen Tiger Ausf.B* (*Sd.kfz.182*), or *Tiger II*, or *Koenigstiger* (Royal Tiger), was in fact a completely different tank compared to the *Tiger I*. It was produced by Henschel from January 1944 to March 1945 in 489 samples (Fgst.Nr. 280001-280489). Also in this case, no specific contracts were signed for the production of the *Panzer-Befehlswagen* version, and this model was mixed in the standard production run. According to a technical manual of February 1944, every tenth *Tiger Ausf.B* one had to be completed as command tank. However, this did not happened, and the first 50 tanks (those with the Porsche turret) were assembled until June 1944 only in the standard combat version. A Henschel production record of September 1944 reported that every 20th *Tiger Ausf.B*, one was completed as *Befehlspanzer*. It seems that in all, only 20 *Panzer-Befehlswagen Tiger Ausf.B* were produced.

Also the *Tiger Ausf.B* was designed to be completed in the *Sd.Kfz.267* and *268* versions, even if the second type was not really of use in the final months of the war, if some tanks were ever fitted in this configuration.

Under a decision taken on 17 July 1944, all the combat vehicles had to be built in order to be converted on the field into command vehicles, according to the needs of the combat units. The *Befehls* versions were realized with the simple installation of the necessary radio sets. The outline was the same as for the *Tiger I*. Normal combat tanks were fitted with Fu 5 radio sets, while those destined to Company and Platoon headquarters had in addition an Fu 2 set. The *Sd.Kfz.267* was equipped with an Fu 5, associated to a 2 m *Stabantenne* mounted on the turret roof, behind the loader's hatch, plus an

Pz.Bef.Wg. Tiger (Sd.Kfz.267 and 268) Ausf. B: specification	
Length:	10.29 m
Width:	3.76
Height:	3.09 m
Weight (combat):	69.8 t
Engine:	Maybach HL230P30 V12 water-cooled 23.8 lt gasoline, delivering 700 HP at 3,000 rpm
Fuel capacity:	860 lt
Transmission:	Maybach-Olvar EG40 12 16B, with 4 reverse and 8 forward gear
Max speed:	41.5 km/h
Range (on road):	170 km
Range (cross country):	120 km
Grade:	35°
Trench crossing:	2.50 m
Step:	85 cm
Fording Depth:	160 cm
Ground clearance:	49 cm
Ground pressure:	1.03 kg/cm2
Power ratio:	10.7 HP/ton
Weapons:	1 x 8.8 cm Kw.K 43 (L/71) 2 x 7.92mm MG.34 machine gun
Ammunition:	67 (gun)
Protection:	hull front: 150-100 mm turret front: 180 mm
Communications:	1 x Fu 5, 1 x Fu 8 (SdKfz.267), 1 x Fu 5, 1 x Fu 7 (SdKfz.268)
Crew:	5

Fu 8, coupled to the usual 1.8 m *Starnantenne D* mounted on a porcelain insulator protected by a cylinder armour welded in the middle of the rear end of the engine deck. In the *Sd.Kfz.268* the Fu 8 radio set was exchanged with an Fu 7, associated to a 1.4 m rod aerial. Extension rods for the *Sternantenne* were stowed in a tube located across the rear end of the engine deck. Other modifications were limited to the addition of radio set accessories (mounts, wirings, junctions, transformers) and one GG400 auxiliary generator set. Room for the radio sets and equipment was provided by the removal of 17 rounds for the 8.8 cm KwK 43 L/71 gun, and eight ammunition bags for the MG.34 machine guns.

About the organization, also the *Tiger Ausf.B* were included in the *K.St.N. 1150e* for the *schweren-Panzer-Abteilung "Tiger"*, issued on 5 March 1943, which foresaw only two *Befehlstiger* (plus one standard *Tiger*) in the *Nachrichten-Zug* of the *Stabs-Kompanie*. The *K.St.N. 1150e* of 1 November 1943 increased to three the number of *Befehlstiger* assigned to the signal Platoon of the command Company, and this remained valid also in *K.St.N. 1107b freie Gliederung (fG)*, of 1 June 1944, and in the *K.St.N 1107d(fG)* of 1 November 1944.

The first *Tiger* units to be re-equipped with the *Ausf.B* model were *3.Kompanie/sH.Pz.Abt.503*, *1.Kompanie/s.SS.Pz.Abt.101*, and *s.H.Pz.Abt.501*, in July 1944. ❏

Pz.Bef.Wg.VI Ausf.H, code "I", Stab **schwere-Heeres-Panzer-Abteilung 503**, Ukraine, July 1943.

This Tiger I of early production had a colour scheme formed by the only standard factory finish in *Dunkelgelb*. Markings include the code "I" (the other command tanks of the battalion being "II" and "III"), in black outlined white, on the turret sides and rear, plus German national crosses, in black and white, on the turret side, and on the side hull. This tank was equipped with Feifel engine filters, and mounted only one antenna, a *Sternantenne D* on the right side, probably fitted to a 2 m pole antenna, as its height was more than the standard 1.8 meters.

Pz.Bef.Wg.VI Ausf.H, code "901", Stab 9. (schwere)-Panzer-Kompanie, **SS-Panzer-Grenadier-Division "Totenkopf"**, Ukraine, July 1943.

This tank was camouflaged with a basis of *Dunkelgelb*, and a mottle of *Olivegruen* and *Schokobraun* oversprayed on it, all oversprayed on the original *Dunkelgrau* applied at the factory. The code "901" was in light yellow (or *Dunkelgelb*) outlined black, on the turret sides and rear, while the German national cross were the usual black and white, on the hull sides and rear. The antenna set was formed by a star antenna on the standard position (right side), plus a 2 meters pole antenna on the turret roof.

Pz.Bef.Wg.VI Ausf.H, code "S02", Stab 8. (schwere)-Panzer-Kompanie, **SS-Panzer-Grenadier-Division "Das Reich"**, Ukraine, July 1943.

The colour scheme of this tank was probably formed by *Dunkelgelb* and *Olivegruen* colours oversprayed on the former *Dunkelgrau* and *Dunkelgelb* finish. The code "S02" (S for *schwere*, or heavy) was in white outline, on the turret sides and rear, while the *Balkenkreuz*, in black and white, outlined black, were painted on the hull sides, and on the left side of the rear plate. The Division marking (the special one adopted for Operation "*Zitadelle*") was painted in white on the right side of the front plate, and on the left rear fender. On the turret there was also the Company badge, a small devil, in white. Also this tank appeared to have only one antenna: a *Sternantenne D* on the right side position.

Pz.Bef.Wg.VI Ausf.H, code "S04", Stab 4. (schwere)-Panzer-Kompanie, **1. SS-Panzer-Division "LSSAH"**, Ukraine, January 1944.

This tank was an early Tiger I delivered in October 1943 with the basic *Dunkelgelb* overall finish. It was then camouflaged by its unit with stripes of *Olivegruen* and *Schokobraun*, and due to the winter conditions, later it received also an ample whitewash finish. The code "S04" (S for *schwere*), in white and black outlined, was painted on the front sides and on the rear of the turret. The *Balkenkreuz*, in black and white, were painted on the hull sides, while on the front left plate there was the badge of the *1. SS Panzer-Division*. This tank was assigned to the famous tank ace Michael Witmmann, and on the barrel it received, in white, his kill markings (88 tanks, in January 1944). It was equipped with a 1.4 meter antenna on the turret roof, plus a 2 m pole antenna on the left side, the standard configuration for the SdKfz.268 model.

Pz.Bef.Wg. VI Porsche, code "003", Stab **schwere-Panzer-Jaeger-Abteilung 653**, Russia, spring 1944.

This tank was one of the Porsche Tiger prototype, which after having completed the test activities, was assigned to s.PzJg.Abt.653, and modified as command tank. It was covered with *Zimmerit*, and wore a three-colours standard camouflage. The markings included the code "003", in red outlined white, on the turret sides and on the rear plate, plus the German crosses, on the turret sides and rear. The unit badge was painted on the right side of the hull front, and on the left side on the rear. Photos of this tank show that it was equipped with two 2 meters pole antennas, probably having received an SdKfz.268 radio set.

Pz.Bef.Wg.VI Ausf.H, code "B", Stab **schwere-Heeres-Panzer-Abteilung 507**, Russia, June 1944.

This was a mid production Tiger I, equipped with a new commander's cupola. The camouflage consisted of light mottle of *Schokobraun* and *Olivegruen* sprayed on the basic *Dunkelgelb*, covering the *Zimmerit*. The code "B" (the command tanks of this unit adopted the codes "A", "B", and "C"), in white outlined black, was painted on the front turret sides, and rear. On the hull sides there was the *Balkenkreuz*, in black and white. The antenna set was standard, with a *Sternantenne D* on the right side, and a 2 meter pole antenna on the turret roof. This tank received also some field modifications, as wooden beams on the hull sides, jerry can racks on the turret rear sides, and a small ladder on the left side, to ease the climbing on board.

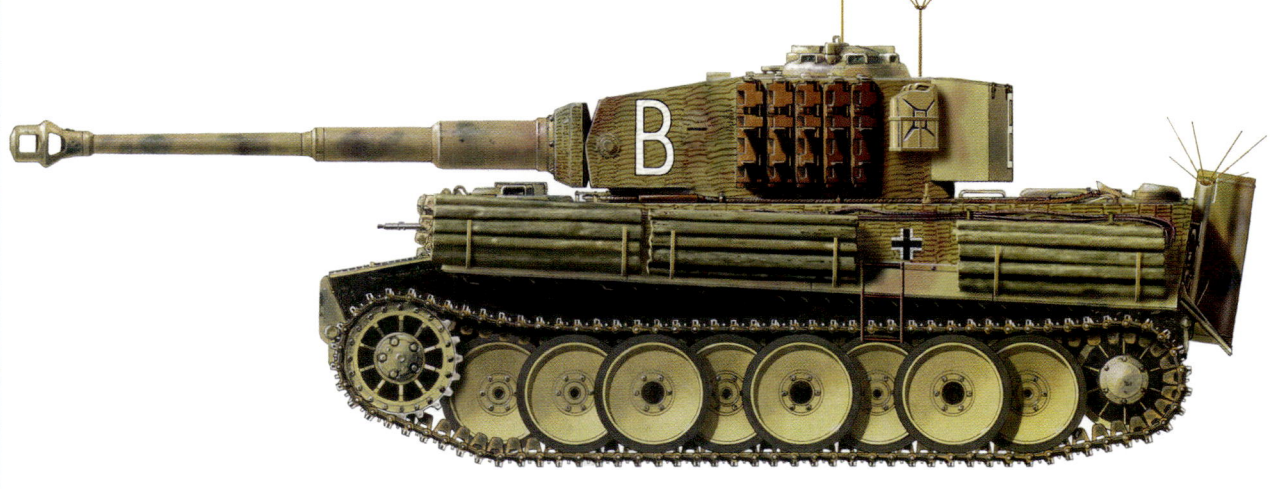

Pz.Bef.Wg.VI Ausf.H, code "S02", Stab III/Pz.-Rgt. "GD", **Panzer-Grenadier-Division "Grossdeutschland"**, Romania, summer 1944.

This early Tiger I (with no *Zimmerit*) had a camouflage of a very light *Olivegruen* mottling sprayed on the basic *Dunkelgelb*. The markings included the code "S02" (S for Stab), in black, on the turret sides and rear, plus standard *Balkenkreuz* on the hull sides and rear. Also the antenna set was standard, with a star antenna on the right side, plus a 2 meters pole antenna on the turret roof.

Pz.Bef.Wg. VI Ausf.E, code "I", Stab **schwere-Heeres-Panzer-Abteilung 505**, Russia, July 1944.

This Tiger I late model was covered with *Zimmerit*, and received no camouflage colors, maintaining only the basic *Dunkelgelb* applied at the factory. Markings included the code "I" (for the first tank in the Battalion HQ) in black outlined white, painted on the gun barrel, and on the back of the turret. The badge on the turret side was black and green, color of the *Stab*. The *Balkenkreuz* was black and white, on the hull side. The antenna set was standard, with a 2 m pole antenna on the turret roof, plus a *Sternantenne D* on the right side.

Pz.Bef.Wg.VI Ausf.E, code "009", Stab **schwere-SS-Panzer-Abteilung 101**, Normandy, July 1944.

Another late Tiger I, this tank was covered with *Zimmerit*, and wore a camouflage consisting of wide mottle of *Olivegruen* and *Schokobraun* on the basic *Dunkelgelb*. The markings were formed by the code "009", in yellow outlined white, on the turret sides and rear; the other command tanks of this unit were "007" and "008". The *Balkenkreuz* were standard, in black and white, on the hull sides. On the front and rear plates there was the *1. SS Panzer-Korps* badge, in white. The profile shows the *Sternantenne D* fitted to the standard position, on the right side, while the 2 m pole antenna was on the turret roof.

Pz.Bef.Wg.VI Ausf.E, code "92", Stab **schwere-SS-Panzer-Abteilung 102**, Normandy, August 1944.

This was a late Tiger I, featured mainly by all-steel wheels, and was covered with *Zimmerit*. The camouflage was typical for this unit in summer 1944, with ample areas of *Olivegruen* and *Rotbraun*, separated by wavy lines in *Dunkelgelb*. Markings included the code "92", in white outline, on the turret sides and rear, plus the German national crosses, in black and white, on the hull sides. The antenna set was standard, with a star antenna on the right side, plus a 2 meters pole antenna on the turret roof.

Pz.Bef.Wg.VI Ausf.B, code "501", Stab **schwere-Heeres-Panzer-Abteilung 501**, Poland, August 1944.

This early production Tiger II was still covered with *Zimmerit*, and received a camouflage of *Olivegruen* and *Schokobraun* sprayed on the basic *Dunkelgelb*. Markings included the code "501", in red outlined white, handpainted on the turret sides, plus the standard German national crosses, in black and white. Also the antenna set was standard, with a *Sternantenne D* on its armoured pot, on the rear engine deck, plus a 2 meters pole antenna on the turret roof.

Pz.Bef.Wg.VI Ausf.B, code "01", Stab schwere-Heeres-Panzer-Abteilung 506, Germany, December 1944.

This late production Tiger II was featured by the lack of *Zimmerit*, and by the presence of a factory-applied *Hinterhalt* camouflage, consisting of *Dunkelgelb*, *Olivegruen* and *Rotbraun* colour painted with hard edges, and covered with spots of the same colours. Markings included the code "01", in red, on the turret sides, plus black and white *Balkenkreuz* in the middle of the turret sides. The antenna set was standard, with a *Sternantenne D* fitted on its armoured pot, on the rear engine deck, plus a 2 meters pole antenna on the turret roof.

Pz.Bef.Wg.VI Ausf.B, code "008", Stab schwere-SS-Panzer-Abteilung 501, Belgium, December 1944.

This late Tiger II had no *Zimmerit*, and a factory-applied *Hinterhalt* colour scheme. The only visible markings were the code "008", in yellow outlined white, on the turret sides, while a black "G" letter was painted in the middle of the front plate. The antenna set was standard, with a *Sternantenne D* on its armoured pot, on the rear engine deck, plus a 2 meters pole antenna on the turret roof.

Pz.Bef.Wg.VI Ausf.B, code "I", Stab **schwere-Heeres-Panzer-Abteilung 503**, Czechoslovakia, April 1945.

This was an early Tiger II, with *Zimmerit* and a camouflage consisting of *Olivegruen* and *Schokobraun* colours oversprayed on the basic *Dunkelgelb*. The Markings included the code "I", in black outlined white, painted on the turret sides and rear, and on the sides of the gun mantle, plus black and white *Balkenkreuz* on the turret sides. The antenna set was standard, while the upper central sides of the turret were uparmoured with track sections, and the commander's cupola received a layer of concrete to its basis.

Pz.Bef.Wg.VI Ausf.B, code "555", Stab **schwere-SS-Panzer-Abteilung 502**, Hungary, April 1945.

This late Tiger II was featured by the lack of *Zimmerit*, and by a factory-applied *Hinterhalt* camouflage. The markings were formed by the code "555", in white outline, on the upper turret sides (and probably rear), and by the German national crosses, in black and white, in the middle of the turret sides. The antenna set was standard, with a *Sternantenne D* on its armoured pot, on the rear engine deck, plus a 2 meters pole antenna on the turret roof.

Befehlspanzer • 87

Radio equipment installed in the German command tanks, 1937-1945

Fu2 EU

One ultra short wave *Empfaenger e* receiver (27,200-33,300 kHz), with an EUa transformer. The Fu 2 was the standard receiver equipment of all the German tanks, from Pz.Kpfw.I to Pz.Kpfw.VI. It was associated to a 2 metres pole antenna (*Stabantenne*).

Fu4 EM

One short wave *Empfanger c* receiver (835-3,000 kHz), with an EUa transformer. The Fu 4 was the standard receiver equipment for the *Panzer* artillery. It was associated to a frame antenna (*Rahmenantenne*) until late 1942 – early 1943, then to a 1.8 metres star antenna (*Sternantenne D*).

Fu5 SE10u

One 10 watt ultra short wave *Sender e* transmitter (27,200-33,300 kHz), with a U10a transformer, and one ultra short wave *Empfanger e* receiver (27,200-33,300 kHz), with an EUa transformer. It was associated to a 2 metres pole antenna. Range: 2-3 km voice; 3-4 km key, while moving.

Fu 6 SE20u

One 20 watt ultra short wave *Sender c* transmitter (27,200-33,300 kHz), with a U20a2 transformer, and one ultra short wave *Empfanger e* receiver (27,200-33,300 kHz), with an EUa transformer. It was associated to a 2 metres pole antenna. Range: 3-6 km voice; 4-8 km key while moving.

Fu 7 SE20u

One 20 watt ultra short wave *Sender d* transmitter (42,100-47,800 kHz), with a U20a2 transformer, and one ultra short wave *Empfanger d* receiver (42,100-47,800 kHz), with an EUa transformer. It was associated to a 1.4 metres pole antenna. Range: 70 km voice; 80 km key to aircraft in-flight.

Fu 8 SE30

One 30 watt short wave *Sender a* transmitter (1,130-3,000 kHz), with a U30 transformer, and one short wave *Empfanger c* receiver (835-3,000 kHz), with an EUa transformer. It was associated to a frame antenna (*Rahmenantenne*) until late 1942 – early 1943, then to a 1.8 metres star antenna (*Sternantenne D*). Range: 10 km voice and 40 km key while moving; 25 km voice and 70 km key while standing; about 50 km voice and 140 km key while standing and using the 9 meters mast with star antenna (*Kurbelmast B mit Schirmantenne*).

FuSpr.f

The *Funksprechtgeraet f* was a radio set with 60 channels, operating in the 19,990-21,470 kHz frequency range. It was associated to a 1.4 or 2 metres pole antenna. Range: about 5 km.

The German tanks and their radio sets, 1937-1945

Tank	Standard Tank	Platoon leader/ Company leader	Panzer-Befehlswagen				Panzer-Beobachtungswagen
			SdKfz.265	SdKfz.266	SdKfz.267	SdKfz.268	
Pz.Kpfw.I	Fu2	-	-	-	-	-	-
Kl.Pz.Bef.Wg	-	-	Fu6, Fu2	-	-	-	*
Pz.Kpfw.II	Fu5 or Fu2	Fu6, Fu2	-	*	*	*	*
Pz.Kpfw.III	Fu5 or Fu2	Fu5, Fu2	-	Fu6, Fu2	Fu6, Fu8	Fu6, Fu7	Fu4, Fu8, FuSpr.f, TornFu.g
Pz.Kpfw.IV	Fu5 or Fu2	Fu5, Fu2	-	-	Fu5, Fu8	Fu5, Fu7	Fu4, Fu8, FuSpr.f
Pz.Kpfw.V Panther	Fu5	Fu5, Fu2	-	-	Fu5, Fu8	Fu5, Fu7	-
Pz.Kpfw.VI Tiger I	Fu5	Fu5, Fu2	-	-	Fu5, Fu8	Fu5, Fu7	-
Pz.Kpfw.VI Tiger II	Fu5	Fu5, Fu2	-	-	Fu5, Fu8	Fu5, Fu7	-

*) Field modifications to transform Kl.Pz.Bef.Wg and Pz.Kpfw.II included the integration of one or two between Fu4, Fu6, Fu7, Fu8, FuSpr.f, or TornFu.g radio sets, according to the needs.